TRADITIONAL ANGLING

By Fennel Hudson:

A MEANINGFUL LIFE
A WATERSIDE YEAR
A WRITER'S YEAR
WILD CARP
FLY FISHING
TRADITIONAL ANGLING
THE QUIET FIELDS
FINE THINGS
A GARDENER'S YEAR
THE LIGHTER SIDE
FRIENDSHIP
NATURE ESCAPE
BOOK OF SECRETS
THE PURSUIT OF LIFE

Fennel's Journal

No. 6

TRADITIONAL ANGLING

By

Fennel Hudson

2017

FENNEL'S PRIORY LIMITED

Published by Fennel's Priory Limited

www.fennelspriory.com

First published in 2010
eBook published in 2013
This extended edition published in 2017

A CIP catalogue record for this book
is available from the British Library.

Hardback ISBN 978-1-909947-22-1
Paperback ISBN 978-1-909947-23-8
eBook ISBN 978-1-909947-21-4
Kindle ISBN 978-1-909947-20-7
Audiobook ISBN 978-1-909947-88-7

Designed and typeset in 12pt Adobe Garamond Premier Pro.
Produced by Fennel's Priory Limited.

CONTENTS

STOP – UNPLUG – ESCAPE – ENJOY

This book, and the series to which it belongs, is about freedom. It's also about the adventures to be had when pursuing one's dreams, developing and communicating one's self, and striving for a slow-paced rural life. It's your opportunity to take time out from the stresses of modern living, to stop the wheels for a while, unplug from the daily grind, escape to a quiet and peaceful place, and enjoy the simple life. Because of this, I'd like you to read it in a distraction-free and relaxing environment: your 'safe place' where you can savour quality time and, if possible, delight in the beauty of the countryside.

That's why the book is pocket-sized, has a waxy cover and is printed using a special waterproof ink. It's designed to be taken with you on your travels. Don't store it in pristine condition upon a bookshelf; allow it to reflect the adventures you've had. Use a leaf as a bookmark and annotate the pages in the spaces provided with ideas of how you will honour your right to 'never do anything that offends your soul'.

The more mud-splattered, grass-stained, and pencil-scribbled this book becomes, the more you've demonstrated your ability to pursue a contented country life. So go on: live your life, be authentic, and always remember to 'Stop – Unplug – Escape – Enjoy'.

fennel

"Fishing is a philosophy. A philosophy of earth, and growth, and quiet places. In it there is a rule of life, a recognition of permanences."

Bernard Venables

INTRODUCTION

Traditional angling is about fishing in a seasonal and uncompetitive way, for the pure pleasure of being beside water. The angler, content to just 'be there', knows that catching fish is secondary to the immeasurable joys of the watery world. By slowing things down, he or she becomes more appreciative of the natural current of life. This, as Izaak Walton described it, enables the angler to become 'compleat'. The focus of traditional angling therefore is on relaxation, peacefulness and tranquillity. It's poetry for the soul, angling for one's dreams.

Traditional angling is also a mindset. It has little to do with tackle. That said, items such as bamboo rods, willow creels and quill floats are crafted from natural materials that make for an organic and aesthetically pleasing angling experience. They look right in their setting, enhancing the beauty and timelessness of the waterside environment. The image serves as a statement to others: that the angler is consciously bucking the trend of what is normal and expected in fishing today. Why? Because modern angling isn't what it was.

Whilst pleasure angling appears to be unaffected

in character, the modern sport (most evident in carp fishing) is obsessed with catching fish. Biggest is apparently best, and if an angler 'fails' to catch then they should hide their shame on the golf course. But it's the competitive mindset that most appals. No longer is angling a 'gentle art', as Bernard Venables described it; it's become a technology-led beast that's more akin to modern warfare. These days, camouflage-clad carp anglers can use sonar detectors to locate their fish, remote control boats to ferry out their baits, underwater cameras to tell them when a fish is approaching their hookbait, weighted 'rigs' to hook the fish on their behalf, and electric alarms – connected to receivers in their pockets (in case they're nowhere near their rods) – to tell them when a fish is attached to their line. I've even heard of aerial hover drones fitted with cameras being used to find the best feeding spots on a lake. Hardly the image of rural bliss that we 'traditionally' associate with angling. But, boys will always have their toys. So if all this technology makes the anglers happy, and encourages them outdoors rather than staying inside to play computer games and watch television, then it can't be a bad thing? Alas, these days, enabled by smartphones and tablets, the modern angler is able to do all that from the comfort of his or her bivvy. They don't need to go home. Or, in the conventional sense, outdoors.

Traditional anglers are likely to argue that the

super-competitive, technology dependent, and all-too-urgent modern angler is so preoccupied with catching fish that he or she is blind to angling's ability to unlock a deeper appreciation of environment and self. As we know: water, in the right light, reflects before it reveals. The modern angler, in retaliation, might claim that traditional anglers are a bunch of tweed-clad loons using out-dated tackle to excuse their inability to catch. But the relaxed nature of traditional angling is deliberate. It's a mindset, remember, about escapism into a deeply cherished world of water, angler and fish.

I wonder what the countryside sportsman 'BB' would make of what angling has become? His classic *Confessions of a Carp Fisher* is one of my all-time favourite books. Published in 1950, it captures the essence of what Izaak Walton described as "the contemplative man's recreation". As a study of the psyche of carp anglers (a new phenomenon at the time), it contains a great deal of mindset and lifestyle observations. Perhaps my favourite of these is contained in the chapter entitled 'The Happy Angler'. It reads: "It is an excellent thing for a man to have a hobby which takes him out-of-doors...I would go farther and say that it is absolutely essential for a man to have a hobby, and the more passionately fond he is of that hobby, the better he will be and the longer he will live. I mention it because many harassed businessmen, thinking of a hobby, would do worse than to take to carp fishing.

But they would need inexhaustible patience and a contemplative turn of mind and should also be of a philosophical disposition...Yet what better time to be out-of-doors than the summer months when our fickle climate behaves itself? And what better way can you study nature, the beauty of trees and water, the play of light and shadow, and the slow changing pattern of the months? ...You may take your tea in peace and quietness and then, as the sky mellows over the heavy headed elms, you will journey forth to your pool once more, 'Wallis Wizard' in hand and creel on back, and discover yet another calm and lovely world waiting to be enjoyed. No small wonder the old monks were fond of fishing."

BB knew that angling is a recreation. It's *supposed* to be fun. So what does it matter whether an angler catches or not? (Or, indeed, that they use the latest gizmos?) If he or she enjoys their day, then that is enough. Which is rather apt, as *Confessions* celebrates its 60th Anniversary this year. 60 years is a respectable lifetime, which makes BB's words read like lifelines to the simple pleasures of how angling used to be.

Most books about angling today are as enchanting and inspiring as the 33-page user guide entitled *How to Lick a Stamp and Apply it to an Envelope*. But with modern angling, there's no stamp, or envelope, just a dry tongue hanging from an eager-looking face. Fennel's Journal is not one of those books. Nor is it

The Haynes Manual of How to Catch Fish Without So Much as Missing a Heartbeat. It, like the traditional angling it celebrates, is a reaction to the cheerless nature of the modern sport. It doesn't take itself too seriously. It pauses to reflect, seeking to convey but one message: that there are a million-and-one ways to enjoy a day's angling. Catching fish is but one of them.

And whilst the gulf between what angling used to be and what it's become has grown wide, anglers know that together they're strong. They fight harder these days to protect our waters from the constantly growing threats of pollution, abstraction, and predation. And they care more for fish welfare, with most fish these days being returned safely to the water. So whether you see modern angling as a declaration of war and traditional angling as a statement of love, both seek peace. As John Lyly wrote in 1579: "the rules of fair play do not apply in love and war".

All's fair then, and enough said. Best we follow Izaak Walton's guidance to "Be quiet and go a-angling".

Stop – Unplug – Escape – Enjoy

When fishing, what techniques enable you to relax and blend harmoniously into the nature around you?

I

TRADITIONAL SENSE

Reverend James Periwinkle sat in his rocking chair and gazed longingly through the leaded windows of his thatched cottage. He stared past roses blooming beneath the windows, past the blossoming hawthorn hedge at the end of his garden, and into the meadow beyond. The scene was bathed in the hazy light of early summer and the air was alive with the flitting of swallows on the breeze. "Today is a fine day," he thought, "a day for fine angling."

One hundred miles away, Dan Flash stood in the kitchen of his penthouse apartment, grinding his morning coffee and staring through expansive glass windows at the bustle of cars and people below. To him, city life was exciting. He loved its social excesses, and the energy and adrenaline of existence. "Today will be a fine day," he mused, "a day for fine angling."

Reverend Periwinkle and Dan Flash packed their tackle and left their homes in search of angling pleasures. The sun was burning the ground by the time they arrived at their destination. Reverend Periwinkle leant his bicycle against a tree and breathed in the richly scented air; Dan Flash exited his taxi and paid its driver. Each man was glad to cease his journey and head towards the shade of the lakeside trees.

"Afternoon, Jim," said Dan.

"My warmest greetings," replied the Reverend. "It is a fine day."

"That it is; I'm glad you could join me."

"On a day like today, St. Peter will surely accompany us. It is meant to be."

A wicker creel was opened and a vintage reel removed from a leather case. A rod bag was slowly untied to reveal a bamboo rod.

"In such perfect conditions," said Revered Periwinkle, "it seems only right to be fishing traditionally."

"But Jim," said Dan, "I always fish like this."

Traditional sense takes many guises, in some more than others. It is a statement of one's belief in old-fashioned values, sparked by an affinity with the past. In angling, it draws the angler towards fishing in a way that feels comfortable and right. His approach may be different to his peers, but he is compelled to stay true to his principles. He may look and fish differently to other anglers, but this is merely an outward communication of his soul, a unique and faithful interpretation of what he senses to be spiritually and aesthetically correct. It defines him. What happens then if the angler's sense of identity contradicts the fashions of the age? What if his beliefs defy the norm? Is he a freak, ostracised for his beliefs, or is he a respected individual, praised for being different? Does he attempt, or want, to fit in? Is he on a different path entirely?

There's been a change in angling during the past fifty years. A change that relies upon technology to catch one's fish. Skill and experience are still required, to a degree, but the advances in tackle and tactics make it possible to circumvent much of the learning curve. This greater utilisation of technology and science has resulted in fishing tackle becoming space age in its design and effectiveness. Angling tactics, especially in modern carp fishing, have become heavy-handed. Up to four rods may be used at any one time. The angling process is automated. It might be efficient fishing, but is it angling? Such lethal effectiveness is a declaration of desperation. It is war at the water's edge. Sadly, this style of fishing is now the norm.

Some will say that in modern angling, the odds are stacked unfavourably towards the angler, that the fish are victims of an assault. So much technological gadgetry invented with the purpose of reducing the need for skill. The biggest change, however, is that modern angling has become too serious. Catching fish has become the be-all and end-all of the act. Individuals seek 'careers' from angling. Wives and children are ignored. For these modern anglers, catching fish is an all-encompassing obsession.

When everything in life is secondary to fishing,

when fish have become the greatest fantasy that a man can desire, it's time to stop calling angling a recreation and time to start calling the doctor. While modern anglers have their target fish, 'top rods', catch rates and pop-up detached homes, a traditionalist's values are gleaned from all that is good from the past. Loyalties, family values, humility, love; such things are important to the traditionalist. It's true that plenty of good exists in present times and ways, and this should be accommodated, but when the fundamental 'logic' of angling has become so alien to the natural sportsman's ethic, what then should the traditional angler do? Those with a traditional sense will follow what their hearts tell them is right. They will fish and live in a manner that feels comfortable. They are just as likely to listen to vinyl records, drive a classic car or write with a fountain pen, as fish with a bamboo rod. There is a sense of satisfaction in being individual, breaking free from the flock to avoid the predictable midsummer haircut. The learning? Listen to your heart, not your head.

Physics teaches us that for every action, there is an equal and opposite reaction: a natural balance of energy that sustains the equilibrium of life. In modern angling, these forces are skewed so far in favour of technology that the balance between science and art is lost. But there is a movement, an undercurrent that defies the flow of progress. There are those who choose not to follow the crowd. They seek not to fish in a predictable, scientific manner. They yearn for the opposite, to buck the trend, to be different. They...are the Traditional Anglers.

The traditional angling movement began in the mid-1970s. It was a deliberate reaction to the way that angling, especially carp angling, was evolving. There came a convergence of like-minded individuals who sought something different from their sport, something that was lost with the advent of modern 'specimen hunting'. They sought to preserve the angling spirit of a 'lost' age, when time appeared to move slower and fish were not 'scaled down' to weights and measures. They were all of a traditional sense, where their simple style of fishing merely reflected their broader outlook on life. It was the natural and only way for them to fish. It was not, as some have suggested, 'an airy-fairy re-enactment society'. Nor was it an illusion or fantasy of a golden age of angling. These men and women were just going fishing – albeit in a way that deliberately contradicted the modern style of angling.

At a time when it's fashionable to appear butch when fishing, when anglers no longer smile when posing with a fish, it's easy to see that a macho mentality disconnects the individual from the softer side of angling. *"Aren't I butch, aren't I hard, aren't I a real man (as I pose here with this 64lb 12oz carp-pig hybrid). Aren't I the man you want to be?"*

It's reassuring that traditional anglers, especially the purists, have the courage of their convictions to express their sensitive sides and be different. And they *are* different. They are eccentrically different. Something that an actor's agent might call "a bit special". Their recoil from modern angling is equivalent to a golfer playing with bamboo-shafted golf clubs, a darts player using feather flights, or a cricket team using a two-stumped wicket. Their behaviour is extreme; it is not for the masses.

The stereotypical traditional angler will use old tackle, such as a bamboo rod and a centrepin reel; they will carry a wicker creel full of artisan crafted floats and tackle; clothing will be traditional country tweeds or a wax jacket and moleskins; they will have a 'defining hat' in a traditional style and a well-honed look of being 'at one' with Nature. Camouflage gear, baseball caps and trainers are definitely out.

Anglers have traditionally strived to use the latest and most efficient tackle and tactics available. Angling, after all, is a form of hunting. If the act were inefficient, then the hunter's family would starve. Traditional anglers, therefore, are not traditional; they are retro. However, modern specimen angling has evolved into the equivalent of taking a machine gun to a duck pond, so where's the tradition in that?

If an angler's priority is to catch fish, then modern tackle and tactics are the most efficient means of achieving success. But traditional anglers, whatever their choice of tackle, are fishing for something else. If they do catch, it is an incidental pleasure. Therein is the soul of the traditional angler: a yearning for a slower, simpler life, where enjoyment is sought more in apparent lack of activity than activity. The traditionalist's old-fashioned approach is often an act of escapism, moving further from the fast-paced, technology dependent, modern world. It's also a journey, like realising that a digital watch (the one that plays *The Birdie Song* at six o'clock each morning) ruins the ambience of the dawn chorus. You buy a wind-up watch as a replacement then realise that you don't need a watch, because you can tell the time by the height of the sun. Finally, you realise that time isn't important at all.

Traditional anglers still catch fish, but it is on their terms, by their rules. Theirs is not, as you might think, a self-limiting crusade. What is sometimes sacrificed in weights of fish is gained in closeness to Nature. It is the goings-on between bites that excites the traditionalist as much as when the float goes under. Indeed, their best day's sport can result in no fish caught at all.

Angling is a sport, so sporting ethics should apply. But if the laws of physics are to prevail, then a balance must exist. Currently, the scales are hopelessly imbalanced. There are six million anglers in the UK, most of whom fish in the modern style. It's no wonder therefore that traditional anglers are so passionate about their sport. What they lack in numbers, they make up for with intensity of belief. To them, nature, angling and life are as one: a union of spirit, counteracting the ailing ethics of a modern world. It is a stone dam, an immovable foundation that supports a watery world and a life spent fishing.

Traditional and modern: can an angler be both at the same time? Is it acceptable for an angler to sit within both schools? Would it be a compromise of personal values for a traditional angler to 'sell out' and fish competitively with modern tactics, or for modern anglers to hinder their catch rate with such antiquated methods? Ask yourself whether angling is meant to be a genteel art, where catching fish is secondary to the enjoyment of the day, or if success is to be defined in numbers and weights of fish? How is your mind swayed? Are you traditional, modern, or a bit of both? Most of us, if we're honest, are both. We enjoy catching fish, and enjoy all the pleasures of being by water.

The most valuable thing to remember, from beginning to end, is that traditional angling is a mindset. It's not exclusively to do with tackle. It is a simple truth: intuition driven by emotion. It doesn't take itself too seriously and aims, fundamentally, for relaxation by the waterside. As Bernard Venables wrote in his *Illustrated Memoirs*, "When all has been said, when all condemnation of modern ways has been declared, there should be a happy marriage of what is old and what is new and helpful. Such has been the case throughout angling's history".

Angling is fun, that's the important thing. Smile, tip your – traditional – hat, and enjoy your time by the water. This is, after all, why we go fishing. Actually, it's more than that. It's an act of faith.

Stop – Unplug – Escape – Enjoy

In what ways does angling support
your image of a contented life?

II

FAITH IN THE FUTURE

In the future, everybody will be 6ft 2in tall, wear ginger wigs and have small funnel-shaped ears. They'll wear foam flip-flops and rustle about in silver jump suits. All the men will be called 'Clive 284' and all the women will be called 'Prudence 81'. They will travel in peanut-shaped hover pods while listening to monotone music that sounds worryingly like Morse code. They shall each have two office jobs, but not work in an office. Their computer screens will be laser-etched onto their eyeballs and their mobile phones shall be implanted into their eardrums at birth. Their faces will be without expression, except on Sundays when the sides of their mouths will twitch at the prospect of eating a green pill for lunch that tastes of 'Spouts 296'. Everybody will be the same, and everyone will be normal. They will have forgotten how to be different, and how to 'Stop – Unplug – Escape – Enjoy'.

How can the future look so bleak when it's ours to create? All it takes is for us to cringe at the thought of wearing foam flip-flops and eating sprout-flavoured energy pills. All it takes is for us to *be different*.

At a time when choice appears to be limited and an angler is expected to produce 'results' from his or her fishing, traditional angling proudly bucks the trend and dares to be different. It has identity. It's not serious, or competitive, or technological. Traditional anglers are not called Clive 284. Thank God for that. Actually, don't thank God. Thank someone much more down to earth.

Once upon a time there was a boy called Chris Yates. He grew up loving fishing and, at the age of 32, caught a fish so large that it broke a British Record: a record that had stood for twenty-eight years. He wrote about his journey and what happened afterwards, and in doing so inspired a generation of anglers to go in search of monster fish that live in secret lakes. He also inspired people to be different.

Chris Yates is the person most associated with traditional angling. His writing made anglers look at the world differently. He opened their eyes to new beauties and the nature around them. He championed an adventurous spirit, always taking the reader on a journey, one where he often shared his love of vintage fishing tackle. Because Chris' writing was so good, old-fashioned tackle soon became associated with the 'Waltonian' angling values epitomised by his relaxed and good-humoured approach to angling.

I am one of the people who identified with the adventure, magic, romance, and excitement in Chris' words (and, I must say, in his photography too). Already a user of vintage tackle, I immediately related to what Chris was saying when he described the 'feel' of cane rods. More passionately, however, I shared his concerns about the "selfish, competitive and unbearably earnest" modern carp-angling scene and the "morose, Rambo tendency" of the tackle fashions which, with altogether too-efficient tactics, made carp angling "as exciting and demanding as playing snap with a tortoise". It was exactly what I wanted to read and exactly what was needed to start a revolution. The Traditional Angling Movement was born.

Of course, Chris was only perpetuating the values already communicated by famous angling writers such as Bernard Venables, 'BB', H.T. Sheringham, Francis Francis and, of course, Izaak Walton. (Also the lesser-known but equally brilliant William Caine, Maurice Wiggin and W.H. Cannaway.) But Chris was writing in an age when the contrasts between traditional and modern were greater than ever before, which made his writing seem more powerful and gave it greater purpose.

While modern angling was in danger of burying itself in a nuclear bunker, Chris made us realise that it is not only okay but positively wonderful to look towards a different horizon where we can stop and smell the water mint and proudly talk about how angling makes us *feel*.

Seeking and seeing beauty in a watery world, and

surrounding oneself with things of aesthetic and emotional value, doesn't define traditional angling. Beauty, after all, is in the eye of the beholder. There's no 'right or wrong' when we describe what is beautiful and what is not. Tackle choice and how we dress is down to individual taste. But Chris' writing, whether intentionally or unintentionally, made us realise that there is a clear distinction between behaviour that is acceptable and unacceptable.

When sporting ethics are ignored (such as 'angling' for fish that are about to spawn, just because that's when they're heaviest), one has to take a stance and choose sides. If you favour a sporting approach, you might wish to put a flower in the lapel of your tweed jacket and skip through water meadows with a smile on your face. Those who don't understand your behaviour might accuse you of being eccentric, an 'overly sentimental Nancy' (as was once described of me). But it doesn't matter. That you feel *and feel comfortable* is enough. Who wants to act in a way that compromises one's beliefs, anyway? Playing safe and hiding amongst the masses will rarely get you noticed (worse still, you might lose yourself in the fog of normality). Be batty, be traditional, and be proud. As Margaret Rutherford once said, "I hope I'm an individual. I suppose being an eccentric is a super individual. Perhaps an eccentric is just off centre – ex-centric".

Being individual and having the confidence to be

different are two of the things that we can learn from Chris' writing. But there is another message, subtler yet more powerful.

If you read Chris' first three angling books (*Casting at the Sun*, *The Deepening Pool* and *The Secret Carp*) you'd be forgiven for thinking that they're about fishing. 'Man goes in search of carp, catches a record, then discovers barbel, moves near to a river, has lots of adventures, then discovers a very special lake with uncaught monster carp, which begins the cycle all over again.' For me, the idea that Chris is pursuing a fish is incidental. What's important is that he's following his dreams (or, as he describes it, "an image"). He believes in his dreams, and believes that if he keeps looking *and believing* that he will ultimately find them.

Unswerving and unquestionable belief? Excitement and encouragement? Surety and resolve? Good humour and eccentricity? Belief in something so important as to pursue it wholeheartedly? All pointing to an unquestionable belief in believing. There's another word for this: faith.

At the first level, you could say that Chris Yates' writing restored our faith in angling. But really it restored our faith in ourselves, to stand up for our beliefs and be different. (How else did a thousand or more anglers decide to abandon their carbon rods and fish like Chris?) Does this make him a spiritual leader? Does it make Traditional Angling the new

Rock 'n' Roll? It does not. The groupies mostly have beards and the only drugs served up are in teacups. And, besides, I don't think Chris would want to wear the loincloth and sandals. Chris' intention was never to convert, merely to open our eyes to things we might otherwise have missed. And he did it very well.

Chris once wrote monthly features for the leading angling magazines; he starred in the hugely popular *A Passion for Angling* series on BBC2, broadcast on BBC Radio 4 and went on to become founding editor of *Waterlog* magazine – a publication for traditional anglers. His activities were broadcast to millions. Many followed his lead; the water's edge was soon waggling with cane rods and floppy hats. Then things went quiet. Why?

A question was raised in an Internet angling forum last year, asking whether traditional angling had seen its day. Several pages of responses were given, each suggesting that 'the movement' was no longer in vogue and was, potentially, in decline. They referred to the reduced profile of Chris Yates and that traditional angling was only ever a fad, a whim of fancy, that all those cane rods that had once been so proudly held aloft were now retired to dusty cupboards. This concerned me. Had the revolution been quashed by a bombardment of Zipp Leads and an armada of bait boats? Maybe the traditional anglers were only savouring a temporary dalliance with nostalgia, perhaps they never truly understood what traditional angling was all about, or was it that they were afraid to stand out from the crowd when traditional angling was no longer fashionable? Was it that they'd lost their faith?

The marketer will say that traditional angling is now a niche market, that only a few hundred people continue to use bamboo rods and vintage tackle. This saddens me (although, as I've said earlier, traditional angling isn't really about the tackle), as I *believe*.

Chris Yates is my friend, and I'm the person he once described as giving him faith in the future. (Back in 1995 I cycled sixty miles to fish with Chris on the opening night of the season. I didn't think anything of it at the time. I just 'borrowed' my landlady's bicycle, strapped all my tackle to it and set off for a new season of adventures. Chris wrote about my antics in *Coarse Angling*, where he said, "Fennel, who is 21, is one of the generations of younger anglers who gives me faith in the future. Not only had his epic bike ride shown marvellous spirit – and a dubious sanity – he'd also kept faith with the old season by dropping out of another syndicate because they wanted to fish all year round".) Chris believed in me, as I believed in him, introducing me to many respected anglers: the 'old guard' of traditional angling, as it were. People like Bernard Venables, Peter Stone and Maurice Ingham became my friends. I felt (and still feel) part of the fabric of traditional angling. I couldn't imagine fishing in any other way. Whilst others may not be waving the traditional angling flag as proudly as they once did, I, and those who believe, hold it further aloft than ever before.

I think that traditional angling has, with the exception of a notable few, merely dipped its head beneath the water for a while. It is still very much alive, there amongst the fishes, but practised in private places beloved of traditional anglers. I'm sure that it will rise again in the future, to break the surface like King Arthur's sword, but for now it's the passion of a minority. A minority who believe in the traditions of angling. They're the ones that, like schoolteachers investing in a new generation, have faith in the future.

III

RETURN TO WOODWATER POOL

Mr Hackney, my school physics teacher, sure knew how to get the attention of his class. "To begin with," he said, "I'm going to ask you to get two bulldog clips, two poles, three feet of flexible curtain runner and some ball bearings. Clip each end of the runner to a pole, and then hold the poles so that they're vertical. Lift the poles so that the ends of the runners are about a foot off the ground and the middle is sagging. You should now have something that looks like a suspension bridge that's melted in summer. Now here's the important bit: boys, you grab one of your balls and lift it as high as you can, then place it at the end of one of the runners. Girls, cup your hands and watch closely. When I say 'go' the boys should release their balls and the girls should observe how far, and how many times, the balls swoop from side-to-side. Okay? Go!" In a fit of giggles, a dozen balls were released; they rolled down the curtain runners, up the other side and back again. They continued to do so until they came to rest in the middle.

"This is all very entertaining," said I, "but what are you trying to teach us?"

"I'm teaching you about energy," said Mr Hackney. "Kinetic and potential energy, to be precise. There's a certain amount of energy in the universe. It cannot be made, only moved around when changed from one form to another. Lifting the ball to the top of the track gave it potential energy, a gravitational store of energy, which was released as it rolled down the track. Galileo created the experiment. It also proves Newton's First Law of Motion."

"Sounds like a load of old balls to me." I replied.

"I beg your pardon?"

"Potential energy might be one thing, but it's nothing without purpose."

"Interesting. *See me after school.* Class dismissed!"

Three-thirty came, the bell rang and several hundred children ran through the school gates, excited to be going home. Except me. I trudged up the stairs to the physics lab where Mr Hackney was waiting.

"Ah, come in," said my teacher as I peered, rather sheepishly, through his door. "I figured you'd understand the message behind the experiment."

"Sir, I've done my homework and understand that 'work done = force x distance travelled'. I get it. Can I go now?"

"Not just yet. There's more to the lesson than that, at least for you."

"What do you mean?"

"I understand, from speaking to your father, that

you are a keen angler."

"Yes, I love angling."

"Good. Then you will understand when I say that, as an angler, you have a force within you."

"What, like in Star Wars?"

"Sort of. You have a yearning to be by water, do you not?"

"Yes."

"Then you are either pulled or pushed towards such places by the energy within and around you. You are unlikely to move at a constant pace through life. Some things will slow you, while other things will quicken you. Sometimes you'll need extra energy and, as you said in class, you'll need purpose to get to your goal. You need energy and purpose to become the person you're destined to be."

"Sir, I don't know what I'm destined to be."

"Sure you do. You're an angler. If you keep pursuing your interest it will lead you to great things."

"How do you know?"

"Because I'm also an angler. Which is why I wanted to see you now. I have something for you – a book. A very special book that contains much wisdom. It's a book that will give you purpose."

Mr Hackney reached into the drawer of his desk and produced a small hardback book. "It's by an author called BB," he said. "The book's called 'Confessions of a Carp Fisher'. It was published in 1950, way before you were born, but I know of no other book that so perfectly captures the allure of angling. Here. It's yours. Take it home and read it. Then study it and decide how it makes you feel. My bet is that you'll want to fish for carp in olde-worlde places, but there's more to it than that, a whole mindset and approach to angling that few anglers these days are privileged to know."

I thanked Mr Hackney for his gift, took possession of the book and walked out of the school and towards the bus stop. I started reading the book on the bus. It was mesmerising. A quiet, slow-paced but intensely atmospheric book. In Mr Hackney's vocabulary, it had 'potential energy'. From the opening remarks of, "This is a book for those who know the hush of a summer night, when every bush, reed, and tree takes on a watchful shadow. When the mist wreathes across the black mirror of the pool, and only the owls, rats, and foxes are awake," to the closing comments of, "I think of Woodwater, of how the stars are now shining down on its broad fine acres, whilst high overhead fly the migrating birds. …if I am spared I will be there once more, beside the pools I know and love, listening to the cooing of wood pigeons yet unborn, smelling the wild sweet water as it smokes in the summer dawn."

It was the chapter entitled "Experiences at Woodwater Pool" that most fired my imagination. Here was where BB hooked and lost his largest-ever carp. More importantly to me, it was located on the Shropshire and Worcestershire border. I lived on that same border. Woodwater could be close. But where? Did it exist or was it a figment of BB's creative mind? I'd have to find out. I had to find Woodwater Pool.

BB wrote that Woodwater was fed by a steam at its western end, was four to five acres in extent, covered in great beds of lilies, and had an island that was a quarter of an acre in size that was thickly overgrown with bushes, privet and yew; it was buried away in thick oak woods, had at some earlier time been a mine, was near to a "not particularly beautiful" pseudo-gothic mansion with a spacious stable yard, had a keeper's cottage within half a mile of the mansion and couldn't be seen from the road because of the woods that surrounded the lake.

I looked at my collection of vintage maps. There was the border between Shropshire and Worcestershire, running from Bewdley in the east to the fringes of Leominster in the west. A thirty-mile stretch, long enough to make the search a challenge, but short enough to make it achievable. I looked for halls with lakes, where woods surrounded both. I found none. Poetic licence on BB's part? I then took an educated guess that the one thing BB didn't invent was his description of the hall (why would he romanticise about something looking ugly?).

A pseudo-gothic mansion? There couldn't be many of those, surely? I had a brainwave. What if I photocopied the chapter about Woodwater and posted it to the local offices of the newly formed National Rivers Authority? Their bailiffs must know all the waters in the area? I sent the letters and, after five weeks, received a reply from a fishery officer in the Severn Trent Area:

"Dear Mr Hudson, We believe the water you are searching for is located on the Berrington Estate near Leominster. While some BB enthusiasts claim that Woodwater is the same lake as Swancoote, the lake and hall at Berrington match BB's descriptions perfectly, although the surrounding woodland has since been restored to parkland by the National Trust. Fishing is not permitted but a lakeside walk is possible."

The Berrington Estate. National Trust. A lakeside walk.

"Mom, Dad, can we visit a National Trust property this weekend?"

The following Saturday saw my parents and me outside Berrington Hall, with me in close pursuit of the tour guide who was sharing information about the estate. I learned that Capability Brown designed the parkland surrounding the hall and that the hall was designed by Brown's son-in-law Henry Holland. The then owner Thomas Harley, who had purchased the land in 1775, commissioned Brown and Holland. The parkland, including the lake, was landscaped first, with the hall built between 1778 and 1781 at a location chosen by Brown. Harley's daughter inherited the estate. She married The Second Lord Rodney (son of Admiral

Rodney) and the estate remained in their family until 1900 when it was sold to Frederick Cawley, who lived there until his death in 1937. Robert, Cawley's only surviving son, inherited the estate and lived there until his death in 1957. (It's probable that Robert Cawley was the bachelor who invited BB to fish at the estate.) When Robert Cawley died, the estate was handed over to the treasury in payment of the death duty. The estate was then transferred to the National Trust.

"And what about the lake?" I enquired. The tour guide responded by walking me into a visitor room adjacent to the stable yard. There she showed me a display of photos of the estate dating from the 1960s and, while doing so, told me of the lake's recent history. She explained that much of the parkland had become a thicket of trees, which had been cleared to return the estate to Brown's original vision. This left only mature specimens in a traditional parkland setting. The lake, she informed me, was managed for wildlife purposes, there being an established heronry on the island. "Every few years we net out all the larger fish and give them to a local angling club, who put the fish into their stretch of canal. This leaves lots of prey-sized fish for the herons." She then pointed to one of the photographs, which showed large pike and carp lying on the ground after a successful netting. My heart sank at the thought of such great fish, with such provenance, being transferred to the local canal.

Berrington Hall was exactly as BB described. It had a bland exterior, almost industrial, like a North of England mill, but with a two-storey portico on the front. To the rear was a large stable yard and walled garden. Lawns spread out from the front of the hall, tumbling over a Ha-Ha and then sweeping down between stands of specimen trees to the lake. And there it was: Woodwater Pool. Its far bank and island cloaked with oak trees; vast beds of lily pads covered the water. Only the nearside bank had been cleared of trees to allow the lake to be seen from the hall. It was so very much like I had imagined. I walked closer. There was the shallow western end where the "black and sluggish stream wound its way through the leafy woods"; there was the island "thickly grown with bushes, privet and yew", and there, on the far bank, "a fine wide open space, almost square, …flanked on all sides by lilies". I imagined BB fishing there each morning and into dusk, casting in his bread paste, wasp grubs and worms, and sitting back to hear, in the gloaming, "the sullen plunge of great carp far out among the lilies". But alas, I'd been told that the carp were no more. Only silver fish remained, left as fodder for the herons that ruled the lake. I thought of the potential of the water, and wished it could be fished by traditional anglers – each appreciative of their surroundings and the heritage of the water. But I was just a fifteen-year-old schoolboy with a dream in his head and a fire in his heart. I turned and began my retreat to the hall. I'd walked only fifty yards when a 'kersploosh' in the lake forced me to spin round and study the water. In the south-eastern corner of the pool, near to a derelict boathouse, was an area of disturbed water. I watched it, and watched it, until my eyelids began to tremble. And there! The vision I had hoped to see – a large common carp leaped again from the water, kicking its tail and crashing back into the pool.

The carp of Woodwater Pool had survived. BB's dream was still alive. It would kindle my passion and shape my future: one that would lead to golden times with like-minded traditional anglers.

I'm talking about the Golden Scale Club. And what a wheeze they are.

Stop – Unplug – Escape – Enjoy

Who inspired you to fish,
and how does their legacy live on
in how you fish today?

IV

A WHEEZE BEFORE TEATIME

It was the last day of the coarse fishing season. Eight members of the Golden Scale Club: Ferney, Demus, Angelus, Skeff, Isaac, Hedge, Max, and myself had gathered to celebrate 'the glorious end'. Our chosen venue was the Dorset Stour. The weather had been kind and we'd enjoyed an eventful day. Breaking with tradition, we'd attempted to catch something. In fact, three of us *had* caught, which was better than last season when the only fish seen was a barely living four-ounce gummy-lipped roach that, we jested, Max the Pugilist had slain with an ugly stick. Today was different. Unusual. Almost embarrassing for a club that's reputed to be eccentric and carefree.

Angelus, the club cake maker, had caught all of us with a home-baked Victoria Sponge; Skeff had landed a drowned sock and Hedge had caught the butt of Isaac's rod as it sailed towards the water following a savage bite.

Of course, we all agreed that Skeff's sock didn't count. Clearly, he'd bent the rules and caught it using a self-hooking bicycle clip. But he was claiming it anyway. And who'd blame him? It was a personal best on the last day of the season.

We'd also done more fishing than usual. Two members – Hedge and Isaac – had turned up before lunchtime and Demus had cast out before finishing his newspaper. Ferney, our somnolent secretary, wasn't breaking with tradition and arrived just after his mid-day nap. I was in charge of the Kelly Kettle. Actually, the four Kelly's brought to sustain us into the evening. This may seem excessive to a novice tea drinker, but not to us. At two and a half pints each, there was barely enough water in them to make tea for the whole day. A gathering of addicted tea-heads should have known better and brought at least one kettle each. Isaac, Demus, Skeff and Max were reprimanded for leaving their kettles at home. Ferney even declared it a Club emergency, saying that if this blatant disregard for one's survival continued then he would have to cancel our account with the India Tea Company.

Once the shock of the 'Great Tea Shortage' had sunk in, Skeff did the maths and calculated that if we rationed our tea breaks to two per hour then we could fish until six o'clock. After that, it was probable that we'd all be suffering from Maddocks' Dry Lip Syndrome. (An unfortunate condition that involves us wandering the riverbank in a zombified state, teacups held with outstretched arms, whilst plaguing people for a snifter of a brew.) Thankfully we all survived 'the parching' long enough to convene at Hedge's cottage at the end

of the day for a much-needed cuppa. The final casts of
the season had been made and calmness had descended
on our group.

Talking outside Hedge's front door, Ferney remarked
at how relieved he was at no longer having to fish for
another three months; Isaac said it would allow him to
paint his bait bucket and Hedge had plans to restore six
hundred cane rods that had been cluttering up his living
room since June. It would indeed be a welcome return
to normality.

The coming three months – known as the closed
season – would be our essential recuperation time,
allowing us to return, rehabilitated, into society.
At first, we'd take things slowly, attempting to tidy away
all our fishing gear from the kitchen and then, once we
were feeling more confident, begin mowing the lawn or
going shopping with our wives. But these three months
wouldn't dictate an absence of Club activity. There
would be plenty to do. It's no coincidence that the
Golden Scale Club Frisbee League runs for just twelve
weeks, beginning in mid-March and culminating
on the 15th June with a final 'fling to the death'.
Rumour had it that Ferney had already been practising,
following news that Max had booked us a challenge
match with the *Salisbury Adult Fling and Swing Society*.
But we explained to him that eight bearded anglers
would have to wield more than an eight-inch plastic
Frisbee to gain entrance to such an event.

That was enough of closed season plans. Although we'd each made our final cast, we still had the evening ahead of us. Any events up until midnight would still count towards the current season's activity. Hedge's cottage would be a fitting destination, especially as there was promise of more tea.

Entering through the front door, we realised that Hedge's home was the very best sort of angler's den. Each room was filled with all manner of fishing-related artefacts. There were nets hanging off every wall, rods stacked in corners, on bookcases and across tables. Every spare inch of shelf space was stacked high with reels, fly boxes, books, creels, varnish tins and spools of whipping thread. He'd even built a wormery the size of a garden shed outside his front door and had converted his downstairs toilet into a 'piscatorial reflection zone'. The latter was a shrine to angling, with mountains of fishing books, a specially constructed rod rack and enough centrepins to keep you 'twiddling your handle' for hours. *A man could go into there and never be seen again.*

Hedge's living room was, as he described, "festooned" with bamboo rods. His restoration projects were strewn everywhere with barely an inch of space for anyone to move. We had to clear the rods aside before we could sit down. Some of us opted to lean them against walls; others assembled them in precarious freestanding wigwam-like bundles, whilst the remainder were rested across our shoulders and laps. Demus, usually the fortunate one, had chosen a seat in the corner of the room and was subsequently boxed-in by a wall of cane. (He was last seen looking out, somewhat dejectedly, from his bamboo prison like a Vietnam prisoner of war. He said that the thought of escape would have been like playing a game of Jenga with his maker.)

Seeing eight Golden Scalers in the same room can be alarming, especially after a day's fishing. Fortunately for Hedge, most of us had abandoned our wellies before entering his home; Isaac had offered to remove his trousers and there was even consideration, once again, of using the so-called 'soap' invention, even though the concept had been dismissed as hearsay at a previous AGM.

The scene was that of typical club fashion: Angelus sat with his back to the room, huddled in the corner attempting to discretely eat what looked like a slice of stolen cake; Isaac was caressing a rather nice centrepin whilst cagily looking around the room, waiting for an opportunity to slip the reel into his pocket; and Skeff and Max were debating how many digestive biscuits they could balance on a turtle. (They nearly agreed once, settling on a number between twenty-six and thirty, but Skeff sparked the argument off again by suggesting that the figure depended on whether the turtle was stationary or moving and how much glue was used to fix the first biscuit to its back.) While all this was going on, Hedge was in the kitchen waiting for the kettle to boil and I was nervously brushing the carpet near to where I was sitting, hoping no one had noticed the maggots that had wriggled free from my coat pocket. Ferney, who by this time was properly awake, was asking for his breakfast and was questioning why a turtle should get to have biscuits before him anyway. Also, he was complaining that the lights in the corner of the room were too bright and that rocks, being rocks, should never move.

Blinding lights and moving rocks? Go back to sleep Ferney. You've not even noticed Demus trapped behind a bamboo screen.

But Ferney was right. In the corner of Hedge's living room stood an illuminated glass tank. It looked like a fish tank but with no water inside. Three light bulbs were working overtime to heat the gravel and rocks below, which, as Ferney had observed, were moving from side to side.

Shouting through to Hedge in the next room, we enquired what was going on in the glass tank. The reply came: "That's my reptilium. Now sod off you scroungers and let me finish making the tea." How very factual he was.

Bingo! Isaac remembered Hedge speaking of this contraption before. The reason the rocks appeared to be moving was because some were not rocks at all, but stone-coloured reptiles lying beneath light bulbs for warmth. Ferney and Skeff, being our grass snake experts and likely candidates for the 'prod it with a stick' Boy Scout badge must have known what the reptiles were. So we questioned them. With their newfound sense of importance, our experts 'knowledgably guessed' that the creatures were Bearded Dragons, or Hairy Lizards or something equally exotic. Angelus, who had now finished eating whatever it was that he'd concealed from the rest of us, remarked that they could be small alligators and that their mummy could be skulking behind the sofa. But the rest of us agreed they had to be Iguanas. They looked too chilled-out to be anything else. If they were wearing sunglasses then they'd have been classed as 'regular dudes'. Like Max.

Of these two 'Iguanasumminks' in the tank, one was laid out and taking it easy. The other was hobbling between the rocks.

"That one's got a limp!" remarked Demus, from behind his wall of rods.

"Nah, it's not a limp, it's a swagger" stated Isaac, as he craftily slipped the reel into his pocket.

"You think he's got problems," said Max, "look here – Hedge has got maggots crawling across his floor; that mummy alligator must have *died!*"

"I don't care," said Angelus, "haven't any of you noticed that there's no front on the tank? What if they're hungry? Maybe we've been brought here as *their* supper?"

Angelus was right. The creatures were not contained

at all and could wander freely about the house, obviously in search of food or, as Skeff speculated, to play on Hedge's computer.

"How many of these things do you have, Hedge?" shouted Isaac, the responsible one.

"I bought five," replied Hedge, "but you only tend to see two or three in the tank at any time; the rest can be anywhere."

After a pause, Hedge added, "Have you seen Spike? He's the one with the bruised foot".

Spike was obviously the one we'd seen hobbling across the back of the tank.

"The name 'Spike' sounds a bit too 'Hells Angel' for our crowd" said Demus.

"Let's call him Colin," said Ferney. "Colin's a proper Club name."

"Worthy of being our mascot," said Isaac.

"And we've just tidied his living room," said Angelus.

Hedge then entered the room carrying our tea on a large wooden tray. He was walking with some trepidation, looking towards the floor. Our makeshift tidy-up had seemingly impressed him and he was studying the carpet that hadn't been seen in months.

"Impressed with the cleaning?" said Isaac.

"No, just checking if it were safe to come in," replied Hedge.

"We don't bite!" exclaimed Max.

"Need to check for my dragons," said Hedge.

Hedge then told us that last time he'd had guests, he'd carried the tea tray into the room only to promptly embarrass himself and his visitors. The first he knew of it was when one of his guests pointed to a noise coming from beneath Hedge's foot. It was a wheezing, whispering "whuerrrrh". He'd looked down, lifted his foot, and seen that he'd trodden on poor old Colin, who'd had all the air squeezed out of him like a punctured whoopee cushion. By some miraculous feat, Colin had regained his composure – and breath – and scurried off to find sanctuary beneath the coffee table, albeit none-too-pleased with his bruised foot.

We gazed over at the reptilium. There was Colin, sunning himself beneath a light bulb like a Brit on holiday. He looked up, saw us all staring at him, noticed the tea tray, shuddered, and then dashed for cover behind his stone.

It seems that the promise of tea is not to everyone's fancy…

Stop – Unplug – Escape – Enjoy

What's the funniest thing you've
experienced when fishing?

V

SEASON'S END

"It is a well attested pedagogic principle," wrote Paul Widlake, "that if you treat people as they are, they will stay as they are. But if you treat them as if they were what they ought to be, they might become what they could be." Wise words from an author whose book is entitled *How to Reach the Hard to Teach*, and sound counsel to traditional anglers who are often looked upon to uphold the sporting values of angling.

If traditional anglers have but one obligation, it is to demonstrate the difference between what is sporting and what it not. If the camouflage-clad hordes do not understand the difference between right and wrong, then it's our duty to show them in the hope that they follow our well-tailored suit. So, shouting from traditional angling's ivory tower, I'm going to share a particularly strong viewpoint: that our actions and values define us, never more so than whether we choose to be a gentleman angler or not.

It was my friend Peter Stone who showed me what it means to be a gentleman angler. "Good morning," he said as I joined him beside the river, "glad you found me. D'you see over there between those two willows? That's the best barbel swim on the Hampshire Avon. I've been baiting it for a while now. Shall we take a look? Okay, approach slowly; the fish will be close to the bank. There! Can you see them? And what about that big one at the rear of the shoal? It must be fourteen pounds. Look at it feeding on the hempseed I introduced earlier. I think today's the day it will be caught. Imagine what it would be like to catch such a fish. It's exciting, isn't it? Right, I need you to do me a favour: go get your rod and meet me back here. I'm not going to fish. The swim's all yours. Be my guest…"

These words were said to me in 1996. I was the overawed twenty-two year-old, Peter was forty-five years my senior and the respected but extremely modest master. We were fishing during a gather of the Golden Scale Club and he'd noticed my nervousness about being in such revered company. "You come 'ere," he said, "I'll sort 'eee out." That's how the day began and how Peter and I became friends. I never caught the big barbel, but I learned more in that one day than I would have done in a lifetime of fishing on my own. I learned what it meant to be a gentleman angler.

A dictionary doesn't do justice to the word 'gentleman', merely describing it as "a man who is cultured, courteous and well-educated". But it's not just a word; it's a way of life. I much prefer the term 'Gentle Man'. This has more meaning; it highlights the qualities that one should aspire to in order to be a good person. A gentle man: someone who's patient, kind, caring, courteous, respectful, forgiving, appreciative, genuine, friendly, smiling, quiet, giving, trustworthy, polite. In fact, all the adjectives you can muster to describe the act of being gentle. Being this person isn't easy. It attracts conflict. There are too many bullies on the lookout for an easy target. A gentle person is easy picking. But being gentle doesn't mean being passive.

While society seems to favour the go-getters (those who 'knock down walls' while 'selling their granny', and who seem to have everything but know nothing), a gentle person is often overlooked as being timid or introverted. I am one such person. But thanks to Peter Stone, I am very proud to be so. I've found that it's far better to behave in a gentle way while quietly building a ladder to the moon (where we may eventually sit in silence and view things from afar) than it is to shout through a megaphone while trampling over all-comers. Being gentle doesn't stop us fighting for our dreams.

I mention these sentiments because I'm in melancholic mood. In fact, I'm more than melancholic. I'm sad. I'm sad that this year marks the tenth anniversary of when Peter Stone left us to fish celestial waters, and I'm sad that another March has come along to remind me that the UK closed season for coarse fish (on lakes and canals) is no more.

The three-month closed season, from 15th March

to 15th June inclusive, once protected coarse fish from angling pressure while they spawned. But with the partial abolition of the coarse fishing closed season in 1995, anglers can now fish year-round for coarse fish in lakes and canals. This makes many anglers very happy.

Big female fish, laden with spawn, present an opportunity for anglers to catch them at their heaviest weights of the year. So they're targeted. But the fish are in a delicate state; they can do without the stress of fighting for their freedom, being hoisted ashore, and doing their make-up for the camera. But it happens, as it's the legal right of anglers to do so.

Doing what's legal will mean you won't get arrested, but it doesn't make it right or gentlemanly to do so. UK law says it's legal for a man to urinate in a public place – so long as he's aiming his pee at the rear wheel of his car and has one hand on the vehicle. (Does this make it right? Try doing it outside a school, or in a church car park.) The law isn't an explicit instruction for the behaviour to become our default, unquestioned, norm. It merely states the bare minimum of what's tolerated. There *are* alternatives, and we have the freedom of choice to choose what's right. The same applies with fishing for coarse fish during the old closed season. It's your choice, but if you knowingly target fish that are spawning, then you have to live with your conscience. I'd much rather you relish the seasonality of angling and fish for something else.

Knowingly angling for fish that are preparing for, engaged in, or recovering from, spawning is agonisingly, desperately, and *morally* wrong. But conservation obligations aside, as a traditional angler it doesn't even seem logical to do it. The old coarse fish closed season coincides with the very best time to cast a fly to trout or salmon, so why fish for anything else? We know this from the traditional angler's go-to reference book: *Mr Crabtree Goes Fishing*. It's a masterpiece of seasonal angling literature, written by my old mentor, Bernard Venables. In later life he educated me about the importance of fishing seasonally, with a black-and-white view that if someone fished out of season then they had not only let the side down, but themself too. He taught me that a countryman is not static like a crow-pecked scarecrow standing in a field; he or she moves with the seasons.

If you look at the closed seasons for different species of fish, it soon becomes clear that there isn't one constant: the dates vary depending upon what part of the country you're in. I quoted 15th March to 15th June earlier, but that didn't apply to the whole country. Devon and Cornwall, for example, never had a closed season. They were too dependent on tourism to prohibit anglers from visiting year-round. And there's never been a closed season for eels, as they prefer holiday romances while clubbing in the Sargasso Sea.

The trout season is also inconsistent. The official

closed season, to allow wild brown trout to spawn, is generally regarded as 1st October to 31st March. But you can start fishing for trout in mid-March on some northern rivers. The trout there, it appears, get their hanky-panky done quickly so they can get up early to walk their whippets. Conversely, the trout of the expensive southern chalk streams appear to be slow and tender lovers. They're still smoking their post-coital cigars in the first or second week of April. The dates in the calendar, therefore, are not as important as allowing the fish a necessary break from angling pressure.

To be be clear: please give the fish a break when they most need it, ideally a three week rest either side of their spawning. This applies equally to spawnings that occur during the the old season. So if you arrive at a lake on 16th June, only to find your target fish spawning, then go elsewhere or fish for something else. Conservation is more important than 'traditional' dates in a calendar.

If you look at how and why the closed season was established, you can see why the dates were wrong from the beginning. The Mundella Act of 1878 put in place a standard closed season for all coarse fish (which, at the time, wouldn't all have been returned to the water as today). But the Act didn't follow the recommendation of the experts, who had correctly pointed out that different species of fish spawn at different times of year, and the time depends upon where in the country the fish are located. (Pike spawn in February and carp can spawn as late as July; and Southern waters tend to warm up quicker than Northern ones.) Instead, it was decided to group all the mud-sucking inedible 'coarse' fish into one category and slap a closed season on them that conveniently coincided with the best of sport to be had from the ultimately more superior and better tasting 'game' fish such as trout. And so species such as pike, carp, roach, bream and tench were given a three-month holiday from 15th March to 15th June. The riff-raff who fished for them were kept away from the water and the well-to-do were allowed to fish undisturbed and unsoiled by the presence their unwashed brethren. And so the traditional coarse fishing season was established. It remained in place until 1995 when commercial fisheries and angling clubs petitioned for its abolition. They were partly successful, with the season for coarse fish being lifted on stillwaters and canals (unless the water was a Site of Special Scientific Interest, in which case the closed season remained). Rivers would continue to be the springtime reserve of the game fishing elite and a few firm-gripped eel fanatics.

The abolition of the coarse fishing closed season on stillwaters and canals caused a rift in angling. Traditionalists claimed that it was unsporting to apply angling pressure to fish at the time when one should be out collecting quills for float-making and digging over the garden in search of worms. Modern anglers claimed that it was a victory, allowing them to sit in their nylon tents all-year-round so that they didn't have to get a job or spend time with their families. And then there emerged – from a plastic bait bucket concealed in hessian – a sort of hybrid coarse angler who liked the aesthetics and tackle of traditionalists but sought to fish with modern tactics. Theirs, it could be said, was the latest evolution in angling. A corruption of one form and softening of another to allow coarse anglers a 'new' form of year-round pleasure: one that maintained the aesthetics of traditional angling while allowing the angler to potentially catch more fish. Boundaries were blurred, and lines crossed. Some of the hybrid anglers chose to go with the new ruling, fishing out of season – and out of sorts. I'm ashamed to say that I became one of them, albeit temporarily.

In January 2003 I was overworked, disillusioned, and on the verge of becoming very ill. I joined a 'big carp' syndicate to distract me from the horrors of my daily existence. It worked for a while; but on the 15th March, the syndicate leader decided that – as carp were the only target species – syndicate members would be allowed to fish throughout March, April and early May. The lake would then close for two months while the carp spawned. I understood and approved of the logic. Losing my sense of self, I went out and purchased a set of four 'long range' carbon rods, big pit reels, electric bite alarms, and a book entitled *Modern Warfare for the Terminally Stressed*. I fished in

March, and April, and Early May, catching all but one
of the biggest fish in the lake. Then the warmer weather
came and the carp began to shoal up in readiness to
spawn. The lake got busy. Anglers caught over a dozen
carp per night. The fish began to spawn and bite alarms
continued to sound. I telephoned the syndicate leader,
asking why the lake hadn't closed. "Sorry, Fennel,"
he replied, "the fishing's too good; we're going to fish
all-year-round." I couldn't believe it. I'd been conned.
Duped into going against the sporting ethic – the
most sacred thing in angling. Dizzy and frustrated,
I realised that I'd lost my way. But it was too late.
The assault had begun and the fish were exploited.
But I had bigger problems to face. Four months later
my world collapsed and it would be the following
summer before I recognised my face in the mirror.
When I returned to my senses, I vowed never again to
fish out of season or compromise my angling values.
I would never stop being a gentleman angler.

I acknowledge that fishing out of season doesn't
bother most people, and that purists will point out that
the closed season was only a temporary thing. (Also
that Izaak Walton stated that April is the best time for
catching carp.) They will argue that if you want to be
properly traditional, then you *should* fish for coarse fish
all year round. But that's not the point. Sometimes
traditions have to be sacrificed in favour of what's
best for the fish. I wouldn't dream of spearing a fish

or using hand-lines like primitive man, even though these tactics are traditional. I am an angler who does his best to be gentlemanly. Bamboo rods and wicker creels only fulfil aesthetic needs. Ethics and values are far more important.

Traditional angling is a mindset defined by purity of intent. It's sporting. It's ethical. It's gentle, caring, considerate and polite. It's not eager, urgent or single-minded. It's seasonal. It's in tune with the countryside, moving with Nature to savour the best of what is available at each time of year. So there's no obvious reason (other than frozen ponds, flooded rivers, and environmental catastrophes) why an angler *shouldn't* fish all year round. The point is that his or her fishing should be seasonal, mixing it up to enjoy the best fishing at each time of year while always avoiding fish that are spawning. For example: fish for trout and salmon in spring; tench, carp and bream in summer; perch, roach and barbel in autumn; and pike and grayling in winter.

As a traditional angler, I 'pedagogically implore' you to be seasonal, ethical and gentle. But for some people to believe me, I'll have to inspire them…with an alternative way to fish.

APRIL

VI

TO CATCH A FISH

I'm writing this on a muggy day in late April. Everything outside appears fixed in a dusk-like half-light. And the air is thick as soup. Water droplets want to form, but a southwesterly breeze prevents drizzle from falling. As an angler, I know that conditions are perfect for fishing. Aquatic insects will be on the move, and the food chain around them will spring into life. Everything becomes either predator or prey, including me as I stand heron-like waiting to make my move.

I should have grabbed a creel, rod and net as soon as I saw the weather. But I hesitated, knowing that I had a magazine article to complete. So I sat at my writing desk, willing my pen to move as my mind kept drifting towards the trout in my local river. Caught between my two greatest pleasures, I became immobile in my desire to both write and fish. I sat and stared at a sheet of paper for over an hour. All without a single word being written.

I knew that I should have gone fishing and taken my notebook with me. But conditions were such that there wouldn't have been much 'downtime' in which to write.

I'd have felt guilty if I missed my deadline, knowing that any fish caught would have stolen my time from a magazine that had commissioned my words. In the end, I decided to stand up and take a walk around the garden. Being outdoors would at least enable me to taste the air and feel the breeze. I'd sense the current of life and, in my dreamy state, swim with the fishes. Or, more likely, I'd end up in my fishing shed surrounded by nets and the stink of previously caught fish.

That's how I ended up here: sitting on a wicker basket in my fishing shed, drinking cups of tea and eating chocolate biscuits while aiming a fishing rod out of the door towards my local river. I'm still undecided about whether I have time to cast a line before nightfall. I know I won't go. But part of me is already at the river, chasing imaginary fish that rise to everything that drifts over their heads. I've been lost in this daydream for some time now. I've pictured a two-pound wild brown trout, a ten-pound sea trout and a fierce-looking eighteen-pound minnow that got confused with a pike when I dropped a biscuit into my tea. It's been the most productive day's fishing I've had in a long time. I think that the next brew will see me battle with the marlin that jumped upstream a while ago, or perhaps start trolling in hope of a tuna. Anything is possible in this shed.

Fortunately for my neighbours, my fishing shed is at the end of my garden. So they can't hear me cursing at losing imaginary giants. (Neither could they hear the commotion of me reeling in their Jack Russell last weekend, which grabbed the pike bung that I 'accidentally' cast over the hedge.) Interestingly, they only see the 'food on the table' element of fishing.

The first question my neighbours ask me when I return from the river is, "Did you catch?" If I say "Yes" then they nod and go about their business. If I reply with a "No" then they look at me aghast, as if I'm about to starve to death. But if I say, "Yes, but I put them all back," then they retaliate with a "What's the point of that? Don't you *like* what you catch? Surely you'd want to *eat* them?" I try to explain that returning fish is a conscious conservation effort, demonstrating a greater degree of fish-affection than knocking it on the head and licking my lips. But they won't buy it. A fish to them is food. Nothing more.

The reality is that very few anglers need to fish in order to survive. We fish for pleasure, not for food. We enjoy the challenge of hooking and playing a fish far more than the thought of sitting down at the dining table to eat it. And then, at some point in our angling life, we find the urge to catch becomes less. We're content to just 'be there'.

Famous angler Richard Walker described the maturing nature of an angler: "At first, an angler will seek to catch a fish, any fish. Then they will seek to catch lots of fish. Then a chosen fish, and finally the biggest fish of their chosen species". My friend Isaac suggests that there's another stage, that when an angler has accomplished his or her objectives to catch the most or biggest fish, he or she will seek enjoyment from helping others to catch fish. I propose a final stage, that it only matters that the angler *attempts* to catch a fish. Doing so brings him or her close to water, to explore out-of-sight depths and reveal mysteries that previously only existed in dreams.

Could an angler go fishing without a fishing rod, line and hook? It depends what they're fishing for. Most people, including my neighbours, think that I'm fishing for a fish. The truth is I'm not. Angling is just a way of relaxing and escaping in the countryside. In that respect, it doesn't matter what or if I catch. I only wish to enjoy my day. If I achieve this then I am successful. Which is why, when I go fishing, I recite the traditionalist's version of The Angler's Prayer:

"God grant me strength to enjoy my day
...And catch those fish that come my way."

A final thought, before we say 'Amen'. Some days I fish in the river, other days I will go to a lake. Days like today will see me fishing from my shed and catching whatever appears in my dreams. All of these places are good. The act of fishing – for fish, dreams or whatever magic is available – is enough. It transports us to a special world where we may cast our lines beyond the reflection of the obvious, into the unknowns of the deep.

VII

THE CUSTODIANS
OF TRADITIONAL ANGLING

Traditional anglers are an eccentric bunch. Why else would we marvel at the bend in a bamboo rod while we test the strength of our tackle against the lunges of next-door's dog? No one could claim that we lack inventiveness – or passion. Our hobby, as much as it sits within a balanced life, can be all consuming. As my friend Andy Wareham once boasted, "I've absolutely got my fishing addiction in check. There's never a day that passes when I yearn to fish for more than sixty minutes an hour". To anyone other than an angler, this might seem extreme. But, as T.C. Kingsmill Moore wrote, "A Man May Fish" alluding to the natural-born permission we have to indulge our hobby.

Indulging our hobby is easy. We just go fishing. But indulging it in a way that completes our desired *image* of timelessness? That takes more effort. Whilst it's easy to refine the details of one's tackle, appearance, and tactics, and select only locations with the right ambiance, it's not always easy to select the right company. There's always the risk that some numpty will appear on the opposite bank and ruin things. Hence why syndicates of carefully selected people are so appealing. We can choose only people like us, who want the same experience.

Whilst I'm keen to avoid accusations of elistism and 'holier than thou' righteousness when it comes to traditional angling, my biggest ambition is to secure a private and mystery-filled lake for the exclusive use of traditional anglers. Together we would relax knowing that we'd secured our sanctuary: a safe place where our cherished style of fishing could be preserved and enhanced, and where time slows to a leisurely halt.

Traditional angling might be a mindset, but the traditional angling *image* is not. If we seek the illusion of timelessness then all the details of what we see around us need to be right. Period-authentic clothing can be ruined if someone wears a modern-styled wristwatch or wrap-around sunglasses with it; likewise seeing a split cane rod fitted with a modern baitrunner-style reel. Get all the details right, however, and the burdens and shackles of modern life can fall away as we step into our dreams of perfection. It's an illusion, for sure, but our ideal image creates and enhances the magic of the experience. Great when we can influence it, but absolutely amazing if we can create it with others. A whole lake or riverbank occupied only by traditional anglers who've mastered all the details of their angling image? Wow, that can lead to an altogether more 'compleat' experience, and memory.

I'm writing, of course, about the idea of 'Canehenge' that I mentioned in *A Waterside Year*. It would be a lake preserved for the exclusive use of traditional anglers who understand the importance of timelessness and traditional angling image. It's been the subject of discussion with many landowners and fishing friends. I've come close to finding and securing the perfect water on several occasions, but restrictions imposed by the landowners (such as not allowing fishing at night) have forced me to withdraw my offer. But now, ten years after the idea was formed, I've been invited to make a formal proposal for the lease of a ten-acre estate lake. It's lain fallow and unfished for fifty years, is wonderfully overgrown, lies secluded in 4,000 acres of parkland, has the backdrop of a magnificent stately home, and – to add to the romance – was once Elgar's favourite lake.

Taking a deep breath, and thinking about the great times we traditional anglers could have together at our own lake, I submitted the proposal to the estate owners. The response was favourable, and the owners now seek to fit my vision into their overall estate plan (which focuses on benefits to wildlife, human access to a previously wild area of the estate, and environmental stewardship). Negotiations are expected to be slow and protracted, given that I'm asking for access to something that's been off-limits for half a century, but I'm hopeful.

Here's a copy of the proposal, shared as my commitment to a dream that will eventually come true.

Dear Sirs

My name is Fennel Hudson. I'm a lifestyle author known for my Fennel's Journal books and Contented Countryman podcast. I'm also a traditionalist who values heritage, old-fashioned customs and natural history. As a Traditional Angler I uphold the 'Waltonian' values of angling – believing that catching fish is secondary to the pleasures of being beside water.

My articles in Angling Times, Trout & Salmon, Classic Angling and The Flyfishers' Journal are celebrated because they champion a so-called 'lost' way of fishing which, by its traditional values and Edwardian aesthetics, is a reaction to the competitive and urgent side of modern angling. Conscientious anglers like me look to traditions of the past as a way of informing a more sustainable and rewarding future.

I, and a group of fourteen likeminded friends, seek somewhere quiet and timeless in which to sit and fish in contemplative manner; where we can care for the environment, indulge our dreams, and call it home. I propose that the lake within your estate would make an ideal venue for this to become reality. Indeed, the lake would make a very welcome home for traditional angling.

The heritage of the estate, with its richness of 'past informing the future', is perfectly aligned with what my friends and I value. The pool's environment and unknown fish stocks would make for blissful 'pioneer-style' fishing. We would work with you to care for the lake, ensuring that the welfare of fish, wildlife and people are balanced for the overall benefit of the estate. Specifically we would prefer to keep the lake in a semi-wild condition, maintaining the magic and mystery associated with a lake that has lain undisturbed for many years. We would not hack out 'swims' from which to fish, or cut vegetation, or leave litter. Car access would not be granted, instead anglers would be provided with vintage bicycles to cross the estate. The traditional closed season (15th March – 15th June) would be enforced to allow wildlife to raise their young in peace. We'd then fish quietly, either from the bankside or from punts, and remain vigilant for signs of pollution, poaching or predation.

Each angler would be vetted and proposed by me. They'd then be introduced to and approved by the Estate Manager. Potential members would be required to display the gentlemanly (or ladylike) etiquette that one would expect of friends invited into the grounds of a private estate. Only those who appreciate the wider beauty of the estate would be granted access. Because of this, I would not refer to the group as a fishing syndicate, rather 'custodians' of the pool and its wildlife. This would give the correct message to members: that their access is granted on the basis that they respect, care for and cherish the pool and its surroundings, valuing the estate's heritage and investing in its future.

Should the principles of this proposal be acceptable, then

I recommend that further discussions and some trial fishing take place. I acknowledge that access to the lake has been restricted for many decades, and as such I remain patient while your stakeholders consider this proposal.

Together we have the opportunity to create a very special arrangement that preserves the traditions of angling and the future prosperity of the lake, appreciating it in much the same way that Elgar did when he fished there.

Yours sincerely

Fennel Hudson

There it is: evidence that the dream is slowly becoming reality. I'll always keep striving, hoping, dreaming of our very own lake: where the spirit of traditional angling will live on. Together, we *will* achieve this vision. So let's always be looking for the perfect water, and the right friends to fish there with us.

MAY

VIII

AN ABSOLUTE BLANK?

Recently I had the delight of meeting one of my all-time angling heroes. He and I were seated at 'The Scribes Table' at the annual dinner of The Flyfishers' Club. As the flight of wine took effect, and just before dessert was served, I plucked up the courage to speak to him. The result was one of the most jaw-dropping and awe-inspiring conversations I could have imagined, about the history and development of fishing tackle and what constitutes a 'traditional' angler. All perfectly in tune with the 'Piscatorum non solum piscatur' motto of the club, that "It is not all of fishing to fish", the conversation resulted in him and me exchanging addresses. Later that week we began a sincere and heartfelt exchange of letters.

My hero, whose arrival at the dinner was announced as "Frederick Buller, MBE", was the accomplished and respected author and historian whose work had inspired much of my angling-related writing. His research into prehistoric ways of attaching bait to a hook, via a fine thread, had revealed that the modern-day (and much criticised) 'hair rig' wasn't a modern invention at all, but rather the rediscovery of the most traditional way of presenting bait to a fish.

Having long-since celebrated his 80th birthday, Fred was able to describe from first-hand experience what fishing was like before and after the Second World War. In his first letter to me, he commented that my views on traditional angling made "a compelling read", and he was curious to know what it must feel like to be known as a 'traditional' angler "when there must be a much more accurate description for the likes of you and Yates and your associates". He'd picked up on my belief that just because an angler uses vintage tackle and dresses in old-fashioned clothing, it doesn't make him or her traditional. He also pointed out that, traditionally, anglers killed their biggest fish (either to eat or for displaying in a glass case), and would use a gaff to haul out their pike. The fashion of modern angling in the UK, which is driven by fish welfare and the proliferation of sporting fisheries, states that it is unethical and often illegal to kill fish that are not acceptable eating or of a size suitable for use as bait for other fish*. And even then, the angler must be fishing in season and have the written permission from the landowner or controller of fishing rights to permanently remove fish from the water.

(Regional bylaws exist, but generally speaking the species that are acceptable to kill for their eating qualities are: salmon – caught after 16th June; trout, sea trout, pike

under 65cm, and grayling between 30-38cm. Those that can be used as bait are fish up to 20cm of the following species: barbel, bream, carp, chub, crucian carp, dace, perch, pike, roach, rudd, and smelt; plus 'tiddler' species such as gudgeon. It is also legal to remove non-native fish such as zander, and ornamental species such as koi carp. Eels and shad are protected, and must always be returned to the water.)

My correspondence with Fred, and the resulting reflections upon the nature of angling, encouraged me to re-visit the book that most influenced my view of the sport. Bernard Venables' *Fisherman's Testament* was published in 1949 and, as he states in the preface, it "started as an escape from a too unpleasant [post-war] present into a wistfully remembered [pre-war] past... Almost anything from that other life was prone to have about it a nostalgic glamour, so how much more so something as intrinsically magical as fishing. It was above all else something with which to conjure into some sort of peace of mind disturbed by a clamorous and nightmarish present...this book is an exercise in nostalgia, a refuge from a very unpleasant period". So many parallels can be drawn between this message and the journey described within my books. A reawakening, borne of dark times and strife, which sought the green pastures of a heavenly-remembered youth; that the simple act of fishing can reveal the timeless beauty of Nature's special places; and where the present can be as rose-tinted as the past.

Of all the chapters in *Fisherman's Testament*, it is the one entitled 'The Mayfly is Up' that best captures the truest beauty of the sport, taking in the seasonal delights to be had during the late spring crescendo of the fly-fisher's year. And, as it's May, we should immerse ourselves in the trill of birdsong, intensity of flower colour and vibrancy of leaves it describes: "At no other time and place in the fisherman's calendar does nature make such a gesture as she does now. These valleys are at all times beautiful, but it is only now that they reach such a pitch of loveliness...To slip away from our daily turmoil at this time to the lush valley of the river is a thing to be long anticipated and dwelt upon. Once having arrived, our ordinary lives slip from us and seem as remote as Nineveh".

And so I reveal to you that my writing is coming to you from beneath an alder tree beside my local river. Water trickles and tumbles joyously to my right, framed by willowherb and iris, each doing its best to out-flower the other. The river is running clear and cool. I can see a shoal of fingerling trout tucked behind a boulder in mid-river; three grayling are poised, shoulder to shoulder in the shady water beneath a willow, appearing as shadows above the bright golden gravel; and a 14-inch brown trout is holding steady in the main flow in anticipation of taking the next fly that it sees. I should be casting to this fish, but my four-weight split cane rod lies motionless in the grass, appearing as contented as an adder in the sun. It waits for the moment when it shall sway back and forth, or feel the judder of a fish. Not now, but later. For now, my being here is enough. I would rather write these words to you than cast to a fish that I could just as easily catch tomorrow. In fact, I'm likely to stay here, pen in hand, until dusk comes and the words upon the page melt into the twilight. By then, the riversong will be mine, and the sky will belong to the stars.

"Piscatorum non solum piscatur." There's truth in these words. In fact, I'll drink to that.

Stop – Unplug – Escape – Enjoy

What words will you write when
savouring the gentle riversong?

JUNE

IX

REAL ALE
AND THE MEANING OF LIFE

Today is the sixteenth of June – a magical date in the angler's calendar. It marks the start of the coarse fishing season. It's when traditional coarse anglers can, with clear conscience, go fishing. I should, therefore, be writing about the collective hope of millions of anglers who are setting forth in pursuit of their dreams. Unfortunately for me, however, today is also the morning after the night before.

It is 10am. Many anglers will have long-since risen and gone fishing; they'll have witnessed their float sinking from sight and held aloft their first fish of the season. But not this angler. I am still in my sleeping bag, wondering why my brain has been replaced by a hula-hooping, hiccupping, one-eyed and surprisingly literate hamster named Gerald who's learning to play the maracas while simultaneously inflating a paddling pool inside my head. In polite terms, I'm feeling a bit delicate.

Last night was a classic opening to the season. Nine of my Golden Scale Club chums met me at our favourite carp lake. We shook hands, talked fishing and got all excited about angling together again. As is tradition, we set up our tackle, baited our pitches, and then left the lake 'to heal' while we went to the pub for some celebratory drinks. We would return at midnight, light a firework and then make our first casts of the season.

Hmm. That's *usually* what happens, but last night is a blur. Gerald, it seems, has painted the back of my eyeballs with his trademark mixture of glycerine, diesel, and popping candy. If we ask him nicely, maybe he'll tell us what happened. Gerald, over to you.

Thank you Mister Fennel, and hello friend. I'm going to tell you what really happens on these 'classic openings'. Last night ten friends – Fennel, Magpie, Angelus, Prof, Isaac, Styx, Rocket, Burton, Phinehas and Demus – decided they wouldn't bother setting up their tackle, or baiting their swims, but would instead head straight to the pub. They walked three miles from the lake to their favourite hostelry – The North Moor – and when they arrived, the evening went something like this:

"Welcome to the best pub in the country," said Angelus.

The anglers wiped their boots and entered the pub, heading straight for the bar. Actually it wasn't really a bar, merely a serving counter upon which sat a cheese and onion sandwich, a cat and a dozen eggs. The cat was the only thing without a price tag so, the anglers assumed, it was either the barmaid or a customer.

"Eight pints of your finest ale, and two of 'the other', please your furriness," said Demus.

"I'm afraid she's a bit deaf," said a voice from a side-room next to the bar. Out came a middle-aged woman who poured eight pints of Adnam's *Broadside* into handled mugs. Isaac and Magpie, the sober ones, received the 'other' – a strange liquid that, due to an ingenious manufacturing process, did not contain alcohol. It looked remarkably like water.

"A toast," said Isaac, "to fishing and friendship." The anglers raised their glasses and cheered, then gulped down the first thirst-quenching mouthful.

Putting ten traditional anglers together in a room with a copious supply of real ale will inevitably result in tales of 'the one that got away' or philosophical debates about the state of modern angling in this country.

"Before you say anything," said Demus, as he finished his pint, "all this modern versus traditional fishing malarkey is nonsense."

"It's true," replied Isaac, "anglers have traditionally strived for the latest and most efficient tackle; we traditionalists are an anachronism, selecting an invented hybrid 'golden age' of angling in which to live out our rose-tinted fantasy."

"Rubbish!" said Phinehas, the purist of the group. "The modern angling scene, with its obsession with soulless tackle developments and devious tactical rouses, is a cold, scientific and results-oriented beast emerging from what was once a contemplative, warm-hearted and simple sport."

(If ever there were a Cold War in angling, between traditional and modern anglers, then Phinehas would be head of the traditionalist's secret service. He often referred to his arch nemesis amongst the 'hairless and chinless' as Comrade Streina – full name Streina Kakkiynapan – which pretty much summed up his disregard for the modern angling scene.)

"Erm, another pint anyone?" said Angelus, sensing it was time to change the subject.

"Shouldn't we be talking about this beer instead?" said Prof.

"It really is a good libation," replied Angelus.

"Aaaah," said Styx, who had just broken into a beer-infused happy place, "that hit the spot."

"You know," said Fennel, with a sense of the moment, "that real ales are a bit like real anglers."

"What, yeasty and smelling like a brewery?" said Isaac, as he stared in contempt at a glass of forbidden nectar.

"No, that there is a parallel between traditional ale, made in the old-fashioned way, that is personal and unique, and a traditional angler who is likewise content to grow organically into his sport through years of careful refinement."

"So your modern angler, on the other hand, is a bit

like a mass-produced, pasteurised lager?" said Phinehas.

"Possibly," replied Fennel. "Lager is very successful in achieving its end goal – a drunken stupor – but is less pleasurable to savour along the way. A modern angler is generally more effective at catching fish, but do they enjoy all the minor nuances of their sport as we do?"

"They're not all like that," said Isaac. "Just because an angler uses a carbon rod doesn't mean they are less of an angler, or countryman; it's just that they're different, and have alternative values and priorities."

"I bet Comrade Streina has alternative values; I bet he wears camouflaged underpants!" said Phinehas.

"Quick," said Magpie, "get another round in before he starts a revolution."

"A discussion then," said Rocket, who had been patiently waiting to accelerate the conversation. "What's your favourite name of beer?"

"Spectrum's *Old Stoat Wobbler*," said Prof.

"Church End's *Pheasant Plucker*," said Demus, keen to check he'd got his teeth in properly.

"Badger's *Pickled Partridge*," said Angelus, "though I'd never drink it".

"Wyre Piddle's *Piddle in the Snow*," said Fennel.

"Harviestoun *Old Engine Oil*," shouted Phinehas, who was keen to rev things up.

"It's got to be Oakleaf's *I Can't Believe it's Not Bitter*," said Burton, "Or Bazen's *The Good the Bad and the Fuggly*."

"The best-ever name for a beer," said Angelus, from an elevated position of knowledge, "is McQuire's *I'll have what the Gentleman on the Floor is Having*, 12% barley wine."

"That's given me the appetite for another pint," said Styx, who stumbled towards the bar. "12% may be strong, but is it the strongest beer available?"

"What about Parish Brewery's *Baz's Super Brew* at 23%?" said Isaac, who should have known better.

"Not as strong as Brewdog's *Tactical Nuclear Penguin*," said Fennel, "a 32% imperial stout."

"A social lubricant," replied Prof, "but not the strongest. We have tasted stronger."

Prof was right. We looked towards Styx and realised that his 'under the counter' home brew *Old and Filthy* was by far the strongest. A concoction designed to unbutton young ladies and unnerve old men, it was ale so lethal that it had to be stored in bleach bottles. Fennel's last encounter with the ale had rendered him unconscious and left his eyesight blurred for two days.

"All hail the Master Brewer of the Thames; for we are not worthy."

"What about pub names?" asked Magpie. "If you were going to open a pub, what would you call it?"

After some discussion, the anglers short-listed four options: *The Laughing Pike*, *The Legered Lob*, *The Trusty Poacher*, and *The Happy Dangler*. But it was

Isaac's *Well-filled Wader* that won the vote and cost him a round of drinks. However, Demus' *Split Ring* and *Happy Blanker* cost him an 'intermediate whipping' and public apology.

"Did I tell you that this is the best pub in the land?" said Angelus, for the second time.

"Yes, Angelus, you did."

"I wouldn't normally approve of such intoxication," said Isaac, "but in the spirit of things, I can inform you that the word 'ale' comes from the Old English word 'ealu' meaning 'sorcery, magic, or possession'. It is, quite literally, bottled witchcraft."

"Ah yes, 'tis true Mister Isaac sir," said Burton, as he raised a wobbly glass, "but ale has been known to solve some of the great mysteries in life."

"Like, are frozen prawns really fish willies?" said Magpie.

"And, can you really get quicker than a Kwik-Fit fitter?" said Angelus.

"Or fitter than a tight-fit French knicker?" said Demus.

"And is it true," said Prof, "that if you wink a hundred times with each eye, then run backwards whilst slapping yourself in the face, that you might look like a complete and utter prat?"

"We're too sober to answer these questions," said Styx. "You lot are falling behind. It's time for another round."

"Beeeeer, the meaning of life," slurred Burton from his slumped position in the corner of the room.

"These living yeasts are a *taste* of life," said Demus, "not the *meaning* of life."

"We all know that '42' is the meaning of life," said Magpie.

"Incorrect," replied Rocket, whilst staring deeply into his mug. "42 is the answer to 'The Ultimate Question of Life, The Universe, and Everything'. However, if you remember your Hitchhikers' you'll remember that no one knows what the question is."

"I know," said Phinehas, as he tried to stand a beer-mat on its edge. "It asks how many boiled baits are required to be placed around the hookbait in a modern carp angler's swim. Answer: 42. Never more, never less."

"Now you're obsessing," said Rocket.

"These are just trifling things," said Angelus. "Don't you all know that the most important thing in life, the most learned thing you can possibly realise, is that the only thing better than going to bed to sleep is going to bed *not* to sleep."

He was right, of course. But then we were all fond of a good book.

"But what about this question," asked Demus, as he held up his pint to the light. "Is this beer going to affect us in the morning?"

"You cannot answer questions in this way," murmured Burton, from somewhere beneath the table. "You have to think of a more creative solution."

The anglers pondered for a while and then Angelus spoke up. "I think I've cracked it," he said.

"Cracked what?" replied Styx.

"I can't remember," said Angelus. "What was the question again?"

"Dunno."

It was then that the anglers realised they were very, very drunk. They could have gone home, but someone decided to order another round. Didn't he Fennel?

Stop – Unplug – Escape – Enjoy

What's your favourite way
to celebrate the new season?

X

THE ADVENTURES OF SMELLY BROWN

It was Demus who first coined the term 'Smelly Brown' after blending up a stinking mess of trout pellets and boiling water. His fishing bait experiment was designed to create a versatile paste that could be moulded around the hook and used to tempt the wild carp of our favourite pool. Once the mixture had cooled, he was able to mash it up into a kneadable paste stiff enough to withstand casting. The process, however, had created such a pervasive stench that he was banned from the pool for a week. The fishy aroma had clung to his hands like a flatulent limpet and, no matter how many times he tried to wash it off, the smell had remained and the "Pooh, that Blummin' Smelly Brown!" catchphrase had stuck, as did the name for the bait.

Over the years, Smelly Brown triumphed as the most successful bait, better even than broad beans, cockles and maggots. The most significant angling events recorded in our diaries were all linked to this wonder bait, even if the captor had attempted to disguise the reason for his success with pseudonyms such as 'Pungent Fawn',

'Whiffy Beige' or 'Stinky Chestnut'. Consequently, our times at the pool became known as 'The Adventures of Smelly Brown'. Here's a selection of some of the stories.

Fish on Fridays

Friday. 9am. Two phone calls were made simultaneously to two equally important gents sitting behind oversized desks in offices fifty miles apart. The first phone rang:

Ring ring, ring ring.

"Yes, Mr Aftermath here, Head of Life Removal and Chairman of the Board of Pointless Tasks."

"Hello Sir, it's me, Fennel; I won't be in today, I've got an upset tum."

"I see, and this is good enough reason to neglect your duties is it? You wish to fail in your passionate commitment to go above and beyond for our cherished customers, to thrill and amaze them at every opportunity?"

"Sorry Sir, I really couldn't make it in; eye of a needle and all that."

"So you really can't make it in then?"

"No."

"Same as last week?"

"Yes."

"And the week before that?"

"I've got it regular."

"A little too regular by the sound of it."

"I should be fine by Monday."

"I suppose you will..."

The second phone rang; its ringtone was an electro dance version of the birdie song:

Diddy-diddy-diddy-dee, diddy-diddy-diddy-dee.

"Yo, Bob Whuppass here, Managing Director of Cashinhand Limited, how's it hangin'?"

"Yeah, Bob, it's Phin'. I won't be able to see you today, something's cropped up."

"Okay fella, see ya whenever."

Silence. Then a third phone rang.

Ring.

"Phin', it's Fennel. Are we on?"

"You betcha; see you at the pool by lunchtime."

"Roger-roger, wilco and out. Toodlepip!"

It had been the same routine for three weeks in a row. Phinehas and I had concocted feeble excuses to avoid work and thus get to our favourite lake efore the rest of our friends. We would have the lake to ourselves and the carp would be fighting each other to be first onto our hooks. As experienced skivers we had, of course, loaded the fishing gear into our cars the night before, knowing full well that our ruse would be successful. We were getting good at it; a cough here, a moment of faintness there, a tummy rumble or two before home time. It was a slick and well-honed plan.

Our two cars cruised confidently and cockily along the deserted midday roads of the West Midlands until converging in a Devon farmyard. Phinehas and I met and shook hands, our look of glee beaming from ear to ear as we acknowledged how easily 'another great plan had come together'. In ten minutes we would be standing beside the lake and in fifteen we could be celebrating our first carp.

"This is meant to be," said Phinehas.

"Better than any amount of boring work," said I. "We are soooo good; the other guys won't be here 'til evening – we will have the lake to ourselves for a whole afternoon."

"Ahhh, the sweet smell of forbidden carp. Almost as good as old Stinky."

"Erm, Phin'"

"What, Fennel?"

"I forgot the bait."

Our journal for that trip said just one word: 'Bugger.'

A Dapper Match

Raap, shlunk, claap. The letterbox made its usual good morning call. First post of the day was always anticipated with excitement, an eternal promise of correspondence from my angling friends. A handwritten letter, a postcard, or parcel of mysterious contents; what could it be? The thought made me run down the stairs as if to catch a glimpse of Santa before he flew back to Lapland.

On the doormat was an envelope, its corners neatly pressed and of vellum wove. "Must be from Isaac," I thought. His attention to detail and fondness of quality were renowned. Indeed, the familiar neat handwriting on the cover confirmed my hunch, but the words on the reverse of the envelope intrigued me: 'An Invitation'. I opened the envelope to reveal a letter written in Indian ink:

Dear Master Fennel, you are cordially invited to fish the very first Dapper Match to be held at our favourite pool. We shall stand in line, in boathouse of old, five of us partaking of merriment, japes and flinging of Brown, then maybe a luncheon by the Dingley Bridge. We shall commence at 12pm prompt, and cease exactly one hour later, in time for a victory cake. A points system shall govern activities, with one point for a Dapper, five points for an Archie Tearabout and ten points for a Lunky Loomer. The winner shall be he with the largest tally (potentially he with a hundred point Tallywhacker), so come prepared for all eventualities. Yours, Isaac.

One week later, the five anglers – Isaac, Magpie, Phinehas, Angelus and I – were standing side by side at our favourite pool, waiting for the turn of noon on Phinehas' fob watch. Phin' counted down the seconds – five, four, three, seven, six, twelve, two, one – and then a harmonious "Geronimo!" was yelled as five baits were cast into the lake. Four floats were then watched with hawkish eyes. The exception was Phinehas' float: an adapted ball cock with the word 'Jaws' written on it, which was being laughed at by all except Phinehas – who knew that only a Lunky Loomer or three-foot Tallywhacker could pull it under.

(Lunky Loomers were the largest carp in the lake, fish over ten pounds in weight that would emerge into your swim as an ominous shadow to 'devour and destroy' all those without the strongest tackle. Tallywhackers were big eels that lived in the pool. Dappers were carp that weighed less than a pound, and Archie Tearabouts were average sized carp of about five pounds.)

"Feeling flushed with success Phin'?" said Angelus.

"Pull the other one, I've got a cistern." he replied.

Fortunately for Phin', all five floats remained motionless.

"Time's running out Phin'," said Magpie, who couldn't understand why we weren't catching.

Phinehas sat down and relaxed amongst the leaf litter at his feet, leaving us standing like penguins on detention.

"What time is it, oh keeper of the dial?" we asked.

"Twenty-to-One," came Phin's reply. "But wait until twelve fifty-five…" as if he'd set a sub-aqueous timer.

A hushed silence fell upon the group as the minute hand approached the crucial time. As if on cue,

Phinehas' float bobbed, then cruised eerily from right to left, passing all our floats as if they were dominoes to be toppled.

"Phin' – you've got a bite, a bite!" we exclaimed, "Are you going to strike or wait for it to pull the plunger?" Phinehas then casually stood up, reeled in the slack line at his feet and then struck into the fish.

We each jumped back as the enormous float ripped through the water, sending a bow wave six inches high. Phinehas heaved against the fish; his rod lurched over and creaked with the strain. He pulled hard, bullying the monster away from overhanging trees and into open water.

"It's so heavy!" Phin' complained, "I can hardly move it!"

"You'd better hurry up," said Magpie, "else you'll be out of time!"

Phinehas hauled the heavyweight towards him, the grimace on his face conveying his fear that the line could break at any second. Masses of bubbles erupted from the lakebed and the rod kicked; we gasped in awe, but the line remained taut. I stooped with the net, readying myself to capture the beast. With a final haul, Phinehas drew his prize towards the net; the water rippled and bulged and up popped…a mud-encrusted log.

"What?" we all shouted, "That was definitely a fish, and a good one too; Phinehas' rod nearly snapped when he hooked into it."

"Stop mocking me and drag it ashore," said Phinehas, keen to catch something during the match. "How many points for a yard-long log?"

I stepped into the water and grasped a black silty branch sticking out from the main limb. I pulled the log up the bank and each of us marvelled at Phinehas' specimen capture.

"Time-out." reported Magpie, but we were too busy inspecting the log.

There, buried into the decaying wood was Phinehas' hook, impaled upon which was a carp scale no wider than a garden pea. "Done by a Dapper," we announced, "Minus fifty points!"

The Curse of the Witch's Tit

It was dawn when we realised that Magpie hadn't returned to our lakeside cottage. He'd been fishing the previous evening and had threatened to stay on into dark, convinced that this was the time when the big fish would be on the prowl. It wasn't customary to fish all night at the pool, but we assumed that Magpie's theory had proved correct. Keen to learn of his news, Phinehas, Angelus, Isaac and I donned our wellies and strolled down to the lake.

We reached Magpie's swim to see him crouched under a broken umbrella. Its ribs were snapped and contorted and its fabric was splattered in mud.

This was the first umbrella we'd seen in use at the lake and, by its state, was probably the last. What caused concern, however, was the condition of Magpie, who was shaking as if fighting a fever. His hands were cupped together and his gaze was fixed firmly at his feet.

"Don't stress," we said as we approached him, "we've not started breakfast without you."

"I need to get away from here, far away. Away from – the curse!" Magpie's response was desperately concerning, if not a little ridiculous. He continued to tell us that his evening had started well, but then the weather had turned and he'd been forced to stay put while an almighty gale thrashed the landscape into submission. The storm had raged all night, with rain and hailstones pounding the earth for hours. Limbs had been torn from trees, and the pool had been whipped into spray that had spiralled towards him, finally crashing down upon his brolly, breaking its ribs and Magpie's remaining spirit. Yet Magpie had persevered, convinced that the elements would awaken the mightiest of carp. But he was rewarded with no more bites, only a tale that would rise to that of legend before the day was done.

"When the storm was at its peak," said Magpie, "when I thought that all was lost, a bough came down next to me that crashed and splintered, sending bark and twigs flying across the ground and flinging this 'thing' into my lap." He then opened his cupped hands to reveal a lump of wood that resembled a rotten cricket ball that had been flattened by a sledgehammer.

"At first I wondered what it was," Magpie continued, "then saw I this..."

We drew in to inspect the item.

"Is that a..."

"Yes," replied Magpie, "a nipple."

"Looks like a..."

"Tit!" said Phinehas, his lips puckering uncontrollably.

"A *witches* tit!" said Magpie, in a slow and reverent tone.

"Don't you mean 'a sorceress's bosom?'" said Isaac.

"No," replied Magpie, "it is what it is."

"So you're telling us that you were freaked out by an old witches tit dropping in your lap in the middle of the night?" said Angelus.

"I guess so," said Magpie.

"Well at least stop caressing it," said I, "because that's just *weird*."

"Well, if it is from a witch," said Phinehas, with a tone of sarcasm, "then what was she doing fishing here? At our lake!"

"I've figured it out," replied Magpie, "she was here, many years ago, in search of carp to use in her potions."

"What, like 'Hocus pocus, bats and stoat, a scale of carp and hair of goat?'" said Phin'.

"It could be worse," said Magpie. "What if she failed to catch a fish and placed a spell on this place; maybe this place is *cursed*."

"I'd be really miffed if I'd just lost a tit," said Angelus.

"I can hear her now," said I, in a deep and sorrowful Welsh accent, "For too long did I angle, and here I did sit, then up I did jump and lose my left tit."

"Right," said Isaac, in an attempt to stay neutral, "if there is a curse upon this place, that is triggered by anyone who would show greed and fish at night, then we need to acknowledge that poor Magpie has been the victim of it. Not only did he miss out on a night's frivolity, he had to endure a violent storm for his misdoings."

"Agreed," came the reluctant response, though our giggles were hard to restrain.

Each of us then kneeled, closed our eyes and bowed our heads as I spoke our peace with the curse:

"Oh withered witch, in pointed hat and dusty shawl
Our friend repents and wishes no brawl
For angle did he as you did before
To catch a fine carp and maybe one more
So before you will curse us and bide us to fail
We'll pierce your old tit with a long rusty nail."

Magpie then stood up and threw the offending item out into the lake. It landed with the faintest of splashes.

A Doctor Calls

Isaac, Phinehas, Angelus and I were partaking of tea and cake and discussing butterflies when Magpie arrived looking especially dapper and carrying a large leather doctor's bag.

"What's with the quack bag?" enquired Angelus.

"It's my new fishing bag," replied Magpie. "My creel leaks when it rains and other fishing bags are just too cumbersome. This is perfect, made in 1927 and still functional."

All four of us gloated at its tanned leather and brass fittings. The 'ooohs', 'ahhhhs' and 'mmmms', were typical of traditional anglers ogling a new item of kit. It was the angling equivalent of young mothers gazing upon a newborn baby.

"You're so lucky" drooled Angelus.

"If only I could find one as beautiful as that" muttered Isaac.

"It's the nicest bag I've ever seen," said I, "and you're using it for *fishing?*"

"Wait 'till you see what's inside," said Magpie, who then opened the bag to reveal all manner of traditional goodies, including a pair of Victorian binoculars, a gold fob watch, a brass miner's lantern and an ash-fork catapult.

"Oh my," said Isaac.

"Deary me," remarked Angelus.

"You've solved it!" declared Phinehas.

"Solved what?" we asked.

"The final piece of the puzzle, why angling is the best form of escape."

"We're no clearer."

"Okay," said Phinehas, "let me illustrate: Fennel, you sit here in your breeks, check shirt and burgundy waistcoat, with an earthenware bottle holding your favourite ginger beer; Isaac you wear similar clothing and a most splendid hat; Angelus, did you or did you not once fish at this pool wearing a monk's habit and sandals?"

"I did, and it was brilliant," he replied.

"And I am here in my spiffingly flamboyant trousers, holding a clay pipe and writing upon hand-pressed paper bound together with string and folded into a leather cover."

"They really are magnificent trousers," said Magpie, "but make your point a little clearer."

"We all use vintage fishing tackle, yes?"

"We do."

"For all of our fishing, everywhere."

"Correct."

"Yet at this special pool we have naturally expanded our fine things to include every item of clothing and luggage, as if we have listened more attentively to the calling; that by fishing here and forgoing our modern belongings we can not only escape to a hidden world, but to another time altogether."

"What, like time travellers?"

"Exactly. Look around us, there is no sign of anything modern here; the newest thing I can see is Fennel's Kelly Kettle."

Phinehas was right. We had subconsciously created some kind of living museum where time seemed to have stopped at a point in the past and had blossomed in this remote corner of the landscape.

"It's not contrived," said I, "we're just doing what we feel is proper."

"What is real and what is fantasy, when our only reference is normality?" replied Phinehas.

"My fantasy involves Kate Winslet bathing in raspberry jelly," said Angelus as he licked his lips.

"Who are we if not ourselves?" Phinehas' question posed a typically deep message. "For without the pressures of our external peers, to conform and adapt to their standards and fashions, we have defaulted to our true selves; it is an unfolding of what might previously have been deemed odd."

"Odd by their standards, not ours" remarked Isaac.

"Precisely," said Phinehas. "Each of us instinctively celebrated the arrival of Magpie's bag; there was no big advertising campaign to tell us we should like it, we just did, and it's wonderful."

"And life is all the better for it," said I.

"Doctor Brown's medicine," said Isaac, "was carried

in a Georgian bag procured by Magpie of Kent; take daily for proper sanity."

And there's our prescription. All thanks to Smelly Brown.

Stop – Unplug – Escape – Enjoy

Where will you continue the
adventures of Smelly Brown?

XI

CLASSIC TENCH

*"Our fishing was quiet; it lay in sweet meadows;
its peace was untouched...about that long-gone fishing
there was ease, an absence of competitiveness, no taint
of striving. ...for me, fishing's real delight lay in its
Eden-like atmosphere, in the blissful hypnosis
of the water's mystery."*

Bernard Venables

Being by water is often cited as being sufficient to appease the needs of the angler-naturalist. Upon reflection, I can see that it is only partly true. Sharing it with others greatly enhances the experience. Whilst time alone can help us to look inward, to fish for things that others can't see, enjoying it with friends can create our most cherished memories. My 'opening night' in June proved that an evening with close friends can create 'the greatest memory we never had'. As my friend Isaac says, "The best catch in fishing is friendship". This is why, once per year, I meet up with my old friend 'Rollo' Breakspear to fish the waters that were once local to both of us.

Rollo's a Midlands lad like me so we head to the waters of the Severn and Teme valleys. Our favourite venue is the estate lake at Dudmaston Hall in Shropshire. It provides our best adventures: perch in autumn, pike in winter and tench in summer. With a large country house reflected in twelve acres of reed- and lily-fringed water, it's a classic venue for the traditional angler.

Our trip this year was for tench, the species for which Dudmaston is most famous. Rollo and I met at first light in a clearing in a wood that breathes life between the lake and the Roman road to Bridgnorth. Here we were able to leave our cars securely, shoulder our tackle bags and walk the half-mile down through the woods to the lake. Rollo walked ahead, he being well practised in dawn adventures, while I clunked and clanked behind him carrying the picnic hamper, kettle, parasol, sunlounger and portable drinks cabinet.

By the time we reached the lake I was huffing and wheezing like a walrus on a treadmill. But my breathing soon calmed as we stood gazing out across the lake, looking through the mist and seeing clusters of bubbles pricking the surface of the water. The tench were feeding, and the lake was perfect. It was like seeing the smiling eyes of one's first love.

I adore fishing for tench. Everything from their portly shape to their strong fight makes them a pleasure to fish for. They're such beautiful fish, too. Their olive flanks and scarlet eyes make them a welcome contrast to silver roach, spotted trout, and golden carp. I also like baiting a swim and awaiting interest from a tench. It's a relaxing style of angling, perfect for an early season trip like this when it's all too tempting to rush things.

Early season fishing is about savouring the newness of everything, which takes time. It's like pouring a bottle of red wine: the end result is so much better if we allow it, and us, to breathe before we drink. Tactics for tench need only be simple, which suits the traditional angler. A lift-method quill-float fished over a bed of sweetcorn is how Rollo and I prefer to fish for tench. But today we would be using lobworms as hookbaits. "The season's a few week's old now," said Rollo, "the tench have wised-up to corn."

We chose to fish the southern bank of the lake, where a line of reedmace fringes the margins. The water drops off quickly so we'd be able to fish within six feet of the bank. With his swim prepared, Rollo cast out while I sat behind him drinking a cup of tea. (I prefer to sit and absorb the atmosphere of a water before tackling up.)

The dawn was perfect: misty and chilled but with blue skies overhead and a copper sun appearing on the horizon. I couldn't focus on Rollo's float for long. Soon I was gazing across the lake at the treetops catching the first rays of sunlight and watching the cattle come down to the water for their morning drink. Soon I was chatting to Rollo about everything and nothing, putting the world to rights while, in between conversations, enjoying the contented silence that can only be shared between friends.

Rollo and I remarked how Dudmaston is the perfect setting for tench, and yet how under-fished it is compared to the canals, specimen lakes and match ponds of the area. We concluded that it was a sign of the times that many anglers prefer to angle where the fish grow largest, or where heavy stocking forces the fish to bite more often.

Just a short drive away, a matchman's horn or a cacophony of electric bleeps would be sounding the start of an altogether more frantic angling experience. Those styles of fishing, and those sorts of waters, are not for us. We prefer to fish in places that are quiet and undisturbed, where we can peacefully watch a float, see herons standing in the shallows and kingfishers dart across the water. We'd seen all of these since arriving (also coots, mallards, moorhens, geese, and swans), and yet most folk would still be in bed. "To rise early," said Rollo, "and experience a dawn chorus beside a lake, is something that everyone should do at least once in their lifetime."

Rollo is one of the original members of The Golden Scale Club (which, as I should have explained, is a group of traditional anglers brought together by Chris Yates – known within the Club as Ferneyhough – during the 1970s). Rollo was first known as 'Rodmaker' (he made a rod called

The Bernithan Beauty which, being identifiable by its black reel fittings, can be seen in Chris' book *Casting at the Sun*) but he was given his new name after years of 'active service' rolling cigarettes for club members. "A craftsman to the end..." he jested.

"Fennel," said Rollo, "as you know, so many traditional anglers think it's all about the tackle, but it's what's on each end of the tackle that counts. Dr Johnson described angling as 'a worm on one end and a fool at the other'. Well here we are, or rather here am I, fishing with a worm. It's a traditional bait, but one that's becoming uncommon in modern angling."

"That doesn't make you a fool," said I.

"No," he replied, "but today an angler is more likely to be described as 'a fool at one end and a hair-rigged Tutti Frutti boilie at the other'."

I thought for a moment about what Rollo had said. An angler using worms today is more likely to be described as a fool, because worms are so unfashionable. Anglers nowadays prefer to use pre-packed baits full of preservatives, colourants and artificial flavours. These chemical pastes are like droppings left by the first super-rabbit sent to the moon. Mixed with eggs and boiled in a makeshift laboratory they become as hard as Dougal McGooliegun, the Glaswegian ship builder famed for driving rivets into a ship's hull using nothing but his pelvic thrust.

"You're talking about Dougals, aren't you?" I asked.

"Dougals are one thing," said Rollo, "it's how they're used that typifies a modern angler."

"Oh, you mean a hair-rigged Dougal," I replied. "The subject of much debate between traditionalists."

(Anglers often assume that a hair rig, where the bait dangles below the hook on a fine thread so to keep the hook point exposed, is a modern invention. But as Fred Buller's research proved, holes drilled into the shanks of bone hooks found in archaeological digs revealed that early man knew the benefit of keeping the hook free from obstruction. But the purist traditional angler believes that hair rigs are unethical. For consider: a fish picks up a bait which is attached to a hook and line; it detects something inedible in its mouth; it spits it out, just like we would if we detected a human hair in a mouthful of food. The hair rig, however, is designed to hook the fish's mouth as it attempts to spit out the bait. Does the angler deserve to catch a fish that would otherwise have evaded them? I'll leave you to wrestle with the ethics of that one.)

"Like them or not, hair rigs are a great way of catching fish," replied Rollo, "but therein is the crux of the argument. Angling is a sport, deceiving a fish by using a hook attached to a bait or lure; fishing is the efficient harvesting of fish – usually trawled from the water with nets. The individual needs to decide if he or she is an angler or a fisherman, and then use the tactics they're most comfortable with to catch their quarry.

The trouble is when the angler becomes too competitive, and ruins everything for everyone."

Rollo explained that his comments were triggered by some recent incidents at a local syndicate lake. "All the carp anglers were casting heavy leads to the far bank, and then retiring to their bivvies to await the action. Few of them were catching. I sat and watched, and observed that the anglers were troubled with ducks diving on and eating their baits. To overcome this, the anglers were piling bucket-loads of maize into the nearside margin, away from their baits. They didn't mind the ducks feeding at their feet so long as the other bank was left alone. I figured that the carp must also be feeding on the maize, so I decided to fish at night, using one rod and a float fished just off the rod tip, and – of course – using maize for bait. It was simple, traditional angling. The carp obliged and pretty soon I was out-catching everyone. Which, I'm sad to say, resulted in all sorts of abuse from the syndicate members. They just couldn't cope with a floppy-hatted traditionalist catching more than them. I had to retreat, leaving the syndicate in search of peace to be found elsewhere. Thankfully we have waters like Dudmaston where the angling is relaxed, just as it should be."

Hearing Rollo's story confirmed my belief that Dr Johnson got it wrong. There's no fool on the end of a line when a worm is being used. The only fool is he who can't share in the enjoyment of others' successes.

It's by angling with friends like Rollo, at classic places like Dudmaston, that reminds us why traditional angling is so appealing. It's not about results or one-upmanship, or even the tactics we use; it's about time spent in natural surroundings, in good company, with a chance – rather than expectation – of catching a fish.

If we're lucky, we might connect with something more magical than fish; we might discover a part of ourselves hidden away in the twilight, seeking the arrival of our new dawn.

XII

A GATHER AT THE DORSET STOUR

*"Fennel, today we were due to meet for our first date.
I arrived at the bus stop at the agreed time, but you
weren't there. I waited, in the cold, for two hours. Then I
moved to a nearby pub to warm up. I waited some more.
And watched through the window. And then you turned
up. Three hours late. Looking as relaxed and unconcerned
as I feared you would. You stood there for ten minutes,
then left. Later you rang me, accusing me of standing you
up. I put the phone down on you. Why? You wouldn't
understand. You never will. Please, for your sake and for
any girl you might meet in the future, get a watch.
You have absolutely no sense of time. At all!"*

Rejection letter from a prospective girlfriend.
November 1994.

One of the things I love about traditional anglers is that,
by and large, we have no sense of time. Some will say
that we enjoy living in the past; others will claim that
we refuse to acknowledge the present and run in fear of
the future. It's true that we nurture a desire to be free

from the clock – to live our lives in a leisurely manner, away from the frantic pace of modern life. Actually, it's more a case that traditionalists have no desire to *quantify* the passing of time. A day can be described simply as 'morning, afternoon, evening, and night' (you may wish to add 'dusk and dawn' to the list if you're arranging to meet another angler). There's little need to segment the day any further, no need for hours, minutes or – heaven forbid – seconds. Consequently, there's a good chance that a traditional angler will be late for an appointment. So if a traditionalist says that he or she will telephone you tomorrow evening, expect it to be closer to bedtime than dinnertime. Which is what happened to me yesterday.

I was lying in bed, just falling to sleep, when the phone rang. Mrs H turned to me, saying, "Do they know what time it is? It's 10.30pm; it's gotta be one of your fishing chums".

I picked up the phone.

"Hey, Fennel, it's Max. Are you joining us at the river tomorrow? We're meeting at Ferney's in the morning."

"Sounds like a plan," I replied, "I'll see you there."

I turned towards Mrs H and said, "Change of plan for tomorrow, I'm going fishing with the lads".

That was how I found myself loading up my car with fishing tackle at dawn and driving a hundred miles to the Golden Scale Club HQ. It was approaching midday when I arrived. (I'd stopped en route to visit Jade Lake, one of my favourite carp pools, to collect water for my writing ink.) Max, Ferney and Demus were waiting for me at HQ.

"Where have you been? We were just about to leave for the river," they said.

I explained my delay and promised my services with the landing net as punishment for my lack of promptness. They accepted, predicting that one of them might catch a slimy bream that would stink-out my net for a week. "Glad to be of service," said I.

Max and Demus then left, and Ferney and I followed in Ferney's car.

Being in the car with Ferney was a relaxed affair, with him driving at a speed appropriate for the narrow Dorset lanes. This gave us an opportunity to catch up on old times. We'd fished together at Jade, but that was ten years earlier. How could time have moved by so quickly? Yet here we were, a decade later, talking of our fishing trips as if they were yesterday. One moment we were discussing the carp we caught on opening night in 1996; the next we were commenting on this year's profusion of spiders and lack of glow-worms.

Listening to Ferney speak made me realise how my life had become filled with so many small but unimportant things: obligations and possessions that obscure the subtle details of the natural world. Ferney has genuine sensitivity for nature. His author's life allows him to slow things down and see, if not become, part of the wildlife around him. For him, every second is filled with excitement and drama – the bird-like twittering of a shrew in a hedgerow; the coolness of an autumn morn; the shapes of clouds; the drama of a star-filled sky.

Ferney's talent is that he is able to cherish the 'now', rather than being preoccupied, as so many of us are, with the 'next'. We were driving along and approaching the brow of a hill when Ferney slammed on the brakes of the car.

"Tractor?" said I.

"No, look!" replied Ferney.

I peered ahead and saw only road, verge and hedgerow.

"Look, up there!" he said.

I tilted my head upwards. There were very few clouds. Maybe this was the source of his excitement? Then I noticed some tiny dots, high up in the sky, that were holding Ferney's gaze.

"Buzzards!" exclaimed Ferney, as if he'd just discovered a new word to describe his excitement. "Ten of them, all circling on a thermal; they've either come together to breed, or they're a family that has yet to go its separate ways. *It's an omen.* You have to believe in omens, especially when going fishing."

"What does it tell us?" said I. "Are we going to soar to our potential, or get covered in super-sized bird poop?"

The buzzards were so majestic, their flights so graceful. They were reaching such great heights with so little effort, spiralling upwards at a mesmerizingly slow speed.

"Man builds a rocket to get to those heights," said Ferney, "while Nature just silently warms the air and allows feathers to grow. How's that for a contrast?"

We sat in silence for a while, watching the birds, then Ferney said "I had a letter from Parker this week. He's been sea trout fishing in the Falklands."

"Blimey, that's a long way from the Avon. How did he fare?" I replied.

"I don't know. He just commented about how exposed and cold it was there. Said if he tried to fish at night then he'd probably freeze to death and die."

"Freeze to death *and* die?" I replied, "Blimey. That *is* serious. Sounds like being asked to dance by a beautiful woman who then drags you onto the dance floor for a rendition of YMCA."

"Very true," replied Ferney, "though I doubt there are any sea trout in the clubs round here."

"Just old trout I suppose?"

"That's not going to help Parker, now is it? I think it's more important to tell him about The Golden Scale Club's imminent name change."

"What do you mean?"

"I thought we should change it to *The Zanzibar Ice Cream Club*. Prospective members would be sent a scoop of ice cream through the post. If it's still frozen when it arrives then they'd get in, if not then they'd remain in the slush pile."

"Literally."

"It would be the best way to keep the numbers down. If applicants got uppity we could just blame the weather."

"And, of course, the letters would only be sent in high summer."

"Naturally."

"And now we've got that sorted, ought we continue to the river?"

Ferney released the handbrake and we coasted down into the river valley. The Stour was in perfect form when we arrived. Its waters were clear and inviting; its weed beds greeted us with a silent wave. Looking downstream, we could see a rod against the skyline. We heard a whistle, then a call for the net. It was Demus, who'd hooked a fish. I responded, jumping out of the car and running along the meadow with my net in hand, tripping and stumbling in the high grass. When I arrived at the swim I saw only a straight rod and a shaking head.

"It's gone!" said Demus. "But don't worry. It was a bream. It would have made your net smell like a kipper's arse."

I apologised to Demus for being late: late arriving this morning, late arriving at his swim, late for when he needed me.

It was my fault. I should have agreed an arrival time

with Max, or set the alarm clock I don't have, or not spent an hour gazing across a favourite lake. I should have driven faster, chosen to travel via motorways, or gripped the steering wheel firmer and snarled at drivers that got in my way. I should have told Ferney not to stop and look at those birds of prey. I should have torn through the mdeaow flowers to get to Demus' swim. I should have...

Actually, no. No amount of disappointment is worth compromising time. I knew this at the start of the day but even more so as I stood beside Demus, who was chuckling at my breathless state.

"That fish," he chortled, "just popped up and flapped around on the surface. And then a pike swooshed up and ate it. And there you were, galloping across the meadow, falling over into thistles and nettles and picking yourself up as though you were coming to save me. I hadn't fallen in y'know. It was only a fish. So *why the urgency?*"

Demus was right. There should be no urgency in angling. As the omen had predicted, we should find a thermal and slowly soar to heights where we may view the world from a new perspective. And there we might find others like us, 'circling' and enjoying being free.

Stop – Unplug – Escape – Enjoy

In what ways could you slow down
your fishing, to appreciate more
of the world around you?

SEPTEMBER

XIII

THE SILENT HUNT

"The Caterpillar took the hookah out of its mouth,
and yawned once or twice, and shook itself.
Then it got down off the mushroom, and crawled
away into the grass, merely remarking as it went,
'One side will make you grow taller, and the
other side will make you grow shorter.'"

Lewis Carroll

Like Lewis Carroll's caterpillar, we traditional anglers
should grab the virtual hookah, muse a while and
consider whether our style of fishing makes us taller,
or shorter. Take last week for example. Having enjoyed
my time on the Dorset Stour, I decided to meet up with
friends who were fishing the Hampshire Avon. Angelus
and Styx had booked a holiday cottage at a lovely spot
where the river flows through mature woodland. I knew
it well, having stayed there before, and always enjoyed
breathing in the dank air of the wood and reaching
down to place my hands upon deep humus-rich soil.
It was one of our favourite fishing spots, where we

would angle for chub during the day and barbel during the evening.

We met up, shook hands, put the kettle on, and talked of old times. Five days later we'd talked, joked, read, eaten, drunk and slept. But not cast a line. We'd followed our usual 'alternative' agenda: rising at noon, feasting until dusk, then drinking and telling stories until first light when we'd close our eyes, open our ears, and be lulled to sleep by the dawn chorus. The Avon fish had been left in peace while the three of us had savoured a slow-paced contented life.

It was the final day of our trip when Angelus and I decided to go for an evening walk along the river. (Styx had become virtually nocturnal and remained in his sleeping bag throughout the day.) We had no intention of fishing; our rods were still in their bags and our bait (cheese, luncheon meat, salami and bread) had been eaten during our frequent 'beer munchies' raids on the fridge and cupboards. The walk, therefore, was intended to be a casual stroll to enjoy our much-loved place.

Walking from the cottage, we noticed how the leaves of the riverside willows were beginning to yellow, and mist was forming in the hollows of the meadows. Most noticeably there was a musky, fertile smell to the air next to the woods.

"Mmm, mushrooms," said Angelus, "time for the silent hunt."

"The silent what?" said I.

"Silent Hunt," replied Angelus, "it's how Italians describe mushroom hunting. If I could find a firtling stick then we might be lucky."

A Firtling Stick, as I learnt, is a hazel or willow stem that's as long as a walking stick but only pencil-thick. This gives it enough flex to flick through the leaves on the ground without disturbing any mushrooms. Angelus cut one from the hedgerow adjacent to the wood and declared, "Let's go hunting!"

This was my first proper hunt for mushrooms. I'd always steered clear of anything other than a field mushroom, knowing that a find could prove poisonous or hallucinogenic. (Once, when walking home from college, I ate some small fawn-coloured mushrooms that I found in the roadside verge. They resulted in me having a perfectly sane three-hour conversation with a Friesian Cow. As I leant on a gate next to her field, she told me that her name was Maud, that she'd recently taken early retirement from the gynaecological department of the local hospital and was now completing a distance learning course in Advanced Economics. Somewhat well read for a cow, she demonstrated an impressive knowledge of world politics, critiqued the attack formations of Premiership football teams, and had memorised the part numbers of an Airfix Spitfire. But she couldn't tell me what day it was, in which direction I should walk, or how to find my feet. Eventually she grew tired of my juvenile babble and walked away, claiming that she was late for a pedicure.)

Angelus, I'm pleased to say, is an expert mushroom hunter who can tell the difference between a Magic Mushroom and one that doesn't produce bunnies from a hat. He carries a special knife with him for opportune moments when the 'shrooms are out. Its blade is sharp on one side and serrated on the other "for removing gunk from fungi". It also has a fine brush at the end of its handle for removing bugs and dirt from the 'gills' on the underside of mushrooms. Angelus explained that a small basket or paper bag would normally be used to transport any finds, but as today was an opportunistic hunt we would 'make do' with the pockets in our wax jackets.

Angelus was soon firtling through the leaves beneath the trees, happily muttering to himself about chanterelles, ceps, boletus, bracket fungi and puffballs. I watched him examine each find, cutting some and dismissing others. Some would be thrown to the ground after Angelus had shown me the maggot holes inside their stems. One mushroom, a purple fungus with a hollow stem, got Angelus really excited. "Amethyst Deceiver!" he proclaimed as he held it aloft. "This can be dried and added to stews."

Soon our coat pockets were bulging with the autumn harvest. Angelus began talking about sautéing the ceps in butter and eating them on toast. I was filled with admiration for his knowledge and skill, which had brought us so close to Nature. But the greatest value of our time in the woods was just that. It was our time, together, in the woods.

It's too easy to arrange to go fishing with a friend and then, after meeting up, spend the entire day apart. There might be the occasional shout across the pool or river announcing, "I've got one!" or an arranged meet-up for a cuppa or partaking of lunch, but the act is mostly solitary. How much better it is to sit alongside each other and talk, making the most of your quality time together. You can discuss, plan and reminisce about things, help to net each other's fish, and ultimately build a closer friendship. Two pairs of eyes on the water will see more, helping each other to spot fish, identify birds and watch for bites. This is how Angelus and I like to fish when we're together. But Styx has mastered it.

Styx is a professional river guide on the Thames. He spends all day in a boat with anglers. His repertoire ensures day-long hilarity and makes the pursuit of fish seem irrelevant. He could offer his boating services upon a playing field and anglers would have just as much fun. On my last trip with him, we fished for pike in the lock cutting beside Marlow weir. I was busy eating a cheese and beetroot sandwich when Styx spoke up and said, "Hey, Fennel, have you heard the one about the blind man who walks into a shop?"

"No," I replied.

"Well," continued Styx, "he walks in, stoops down

and grabs his Labrador guide dog by its hind legs, lifts it up and then starts swinging the dog round and round, higher and higher until its eyes are bulging, its tongue is hanging from its mouth and the animal is spinning at shoulder height to him. The shopkeeper, who is somewhat perplexed by the spectacle, asks the blind man if he's okay. 'Are you alright?' he enquires, 'May I be of any assistance?' 'No, I'm quite okay,' replies the blind man, 'I'm just having a look around...'"

The joke was typical of Styx's sense of humour and his desire for anglers to have an eventful and enjoyable day.

Angelus and I decided that we'd left Styx alone in the cottage for long enough. We looked up from the woodland floor and stared through the gloom to the warm evening light bathing the water meadow beyond the wood.

"The barbel must surely be feeding?" Said I. "Should we fetch our rods?"

"No," replied Angelus, "we have no bait, and besides, wouldn't you rather we ate a late breakfast? Bacon, sausage, and a large mug of tea would go rather well with these mushrooms, don't you think?"

Angelus was right. The mushrooms would be delicious and we were keen for Styx to wake to the sound of a boiling kettle. I knew, right then, that the Silent Hunt would become an integral part of our time by the river. But it was friendship that made it worthwhile.

Angling, it seemed, had extended beyond the boundaries of a watery world to grow up from the leaves of the woodland floor. All part of the slow and organic cycle of life that, by encouraging us to look closer, had made our lives more complete. But of course, there are many sides to every story...

Stop – Unplug – Escape – Enjoy

What do you seek
when you go fishing?

XIV

SIX SIDES TO EVERY STORY

I need to make a confession: I am suffering from what my friend Isaac would describe as "a libation too many". You'd have thought that I'd have learned my lesson back in June. But for the past three hours, as I've stayed up late writing my journals, I've been taking a sip (okay, a glug) of port with each completed page. Like the sands of time that fall through an hourglass, the journals filled as the port bottles depleted. I managed a ratio of 1:1. And then I saw, rather blurrily, three filled journals and three empty bottles. Impressed by my creativity and stamina, I realised that I needed 'output' of another kind. I attempted to stand up to walk to the loo, but found that my legs had unscrewed themselves and gone to bed. I prodded my lower back. It was numb. I tried to move my chair. It croaked like a disapproving toad. I looked around the room. Everything was swirling in a blurring, dizzying array of kaleidoscopic randomness. It led me to a conclusion: that I might possibly be just a little bit drunk.

If I close my left eye, and stare very hard at the nib of my pen, I can stop its psychedelic dance.

Presented as a single static image, I know that the nib will not bend like a paintbrush and melt into the page as I attempt to write. But unlike most alcohol-induced inebriations, my condition is port-induced which means that although my body wants to float around the room to the tune of Sgt Pepper, my mind is still relatively 'with it'. So I'm going to attempt to complete this chapter before I collapse in my chair and request the assistance of an emergency kebab.

Let us get things straight: this book is themed around traditional angling, yes? Good. At least I can remember that bit. And I've communicated how it can enhance the quality of our angling lives? Excellent. And I've mentioned about mindset? Okay. What else is there to discuss? Hmm. Given my current state, I'm going to loosen the reins a bit and see where this rubber-nibbed pen takes us. Let's go for the big one. Let's talk about, or rather 'tackle', the subject of bamboo rods.

I might soberly harp on about traditional angling being nothing to do with tackle and everything to do with mindset, but I have as much desire to use modern gear as a hedgehog has of carrying a reflective sign saying 'motorists aim here'. Sure, I use it when required, but I prefer classically styled tackle. Traditional fishing tackle should, to me at least, have a vintage look, be skilfully handcrafted and, if possible, be quirky. It doesn't have to perform super-efficiently – the creaks of an old cane rod or the clunks of a well-used reel merely add to their character. The use of natural materials in the construction of a fishing rod makes for an experience that is in keeping with nature and in tune with the angling of our forefathers. Such materials have the right aesthetic. We can gaze at the rod and, for a while, convince ourselves that we have stepped outside of time, to connect more completely with the slow-moving world of water. It's a way of breathing deeply when we're otherwise short of breath. But traditional anglers are a batty bunch. We're barking mad, bonkers, eccentric. We're mavericks who enjoy hindering our chances of catching fish by using clapped-out tackle and antiquated techniques. We haven't a chance of reeling in a fifty-pound sabre-toothed gudgeon while simultaneously polishing off a six-pack of lager. We are the minority, the ones making a difference by being different. Together we are strong, showing more pride than could be achieved by any amount of bleeps from an electronic 'sindicator'.

Cor. That sounds like a Presidential speech. I'll save it for the next time I stand on a podium. Which, given the state of my legs, won't be any time soon. Best I get back to talking about rods.

Most aficionados of split cane bamboo rods will argue that the carbon equivalent has a feeling of soulless factory production, being finished with rubberised foam or shrink-tube handles, plastic reel fittings, black rings and whippings, and 'eee-poxy!' varnish. All of these elements contribute to a feeling of cheapness and poor quality. Some handmade and top-end carbon rods succeed in breaking the rule, but in the main, using a carbon rod is like eating a microwave ready meal from a plastic tray. Functional, yes, but aesthetic and soulful it is not.

A fishing rod should, whenever possible, be made from split cane bamboo, have cork handles, metal ferrules, silk whippings, and silver or bronze-coloured rings. Bamboo rods like this look right in a natural setting; they feel right and have the reassurance of being lovingly made by a skilled craftsman. The slick, modern equivalent doesn't sit comfortably in traditional surroundings. It gnaws at the traditional sense, piercing one's eyes like a carbon splinter. (Nearly as bad as resting a bamboo rod on a stainless steel 'rod pod', which is about as appealing as seeing a Model-T Ford fitted with 'fat boy' alloy wheels.) Asking a traditionalist to use a carbon rod is like asking an artist to paint with a toilet brush. (Or worse, asking them to sit beside a photocopier while it spits out flat, lifeless facsimiles of their once-great work.) Pick up a carbon rod, wave it in the air, and you'll realise it has the sensory appeal of a methane-filled drainpipe. Carbon rods are too light, too mass-produced and too 'damn ugly'. They are as black and lifeless as the Grim Reaper's underpants.

A well-crafted bamboo rod, on the other hand, is the traditional angler's wand. Very much the symbol of traditional angling, it is the most aesthetically pleasing, sensitive, nostalgic and 'communicative' of all items of tackle. When swishing one through the air, the angler can almost hear the "Shhh" of Izaak Walton as he reminds us to "Study to be Quiet". So much magic in something that was once a super-sized grass, which was split and reassembled as a six-sided fishing rod.

Many authors have written about the appeal of bamboo rods, but they have all, it seems, overlooked the most important subject of all: the real reason why split cane rods are six-sided. I'm looking (with one eye) at my rods at the moment. There are thirty-eight of them, each hanging in its bag from a shelf near to my desk. I'm going to think about their history and character, then decide the purpose of each side of their hexagonal construction. So here goes:

Each and every cane rod begins life as a mighty bamboo plant. The best of these grow in the Guangdong Province of China, where the finest plants shoot from a defined place upon the mountain. Here, the temperature, wind, rainfall, light and humidity are perfect to ensure the bamboo grows straight and fast. When the bamboo grows to the appropriate height it is felled by the villagers and carried down the mountain where it is bundled, dried, and sent for shipping where it will spend up to six months at sea. The bamboo supports a local community. Their livelihoods depend on its growth. The rod that was once living, sustained the life of so many. Considering this, I determine that the first side of the rod, the one that faces upwards in use, represents *life*.

The rodmaker, who ordered the culms of bamboo, selects them carefully to avoid any imperfections that might impede performance of the rod. He will then cure the cane over heat, split it and gently plane each strip until the exact taper for the rod is achieved. He will then glue the six strips together, fix the metal ferrules and cork handles, whip the rings to the cane and varnish the rod for a glassy finish. It sounds straightforward, but it's not. Far from it. A rodmaker who builds with cane is a master craftsman working to precise tolerances; his workmanship needs to be of the highest standard because it's scrutinised by the most discerning of customers. The second side of the rod, moving clockwise, represents *skill*.

The angler who ordered the rod will probably have waited eighteen months or more for it to arrive; such is the demand for rods made by a master. But this matters not. The angler's yearning for the rod will grow by the day; he or she will imagine opening its protective tube, breathing in the syrupy aroma of the fresh varnish, stroking the silky-smooth cork, holding the rod in their hand, casting it and feeling its fibres flex. With every day their love for the rod will grow. The third side of the rod signifies the angler's *passion*.

A growing season on a mountainside, months at sea, weeks of skilful crafting by the rod builder, a year or more of waiting for the order to be complete. So much waiting for perfection. The fourth side of the rod symbolizes *patience*.

When the rod is first used, the angler will fish with newfound confidence, sure that the rod will perform admirably with every cast and with each fish played to the net. The qualities of the rod will be obvious, and he or she will be proud to use it. There will be those who mock the choice of rod. "It is so heavy, so floppy; unable to cast great distances or with heavy weights." The angler will not care. He or she has courage of conviction. His or her determination will be as strong as the rod itself, both of which shall endure. The fifth side represents *strength*.

The angler shall cherish the rod for all their years. It may even become their favourite. When his or her days end, the rod will be passed to a special relative or friend. "A favourite rod, bequeathed with love." But it is more than just a rod; it represents the life of the angler. It will become an inherited treasure, a family heirloom, a gift for a new generation, to continue fishing and by doing so, adding to a lifetime of memories. The sixth and final side represents *legacy*.

Six sides: Life, Skill, Passion, Patience, Strength, and Legacy. Together they represent the value of a cane rod and the resolve of the angler who uses it. Sadly, it's truth that not everyone sees.

Stop – Unplug – Escape – Enjoy

Which of your fishing rods contains,
and weaves, the most magic?

XV

ANGLER'S DISPATCH

My friend, we have a situation. A letter has arrived at Priory HQ. If I'm reading it correctly, it is a declaration of war against traditional anglers. Written in red Biro on lined paper, it was sent via second-class mail by a man who, for the sake of anonymity, shall be called Mr Wayne Tipple of 56 Greyhound Lane, Chigwell, Essex. It reads:

"You and you're fishin crownies wanna live in the past but its gone and you never gorna get it back so you wastin yur time doin whatyou do you lusers you shud pack it in cos nobodies intrested and its all gonna corlaps and when it dos I will be their laffin at ya"

Interesting. It seems we have a challenger, of sorts. Which presents us with an opportunity.

Firstly, we should decide how to respond to the offender; secondly, we should have an off-the-record chat about some of his more informed observations; and thirdly we should write a response. Sounds like a plan? Good. Then let's get the kettle on and meet back here in a few minutes, armed with the essentials of traditional warfare.

Okay. I'm back. I have a cup of tea in one hand and my thickest-nibbed fountain pen in the other. So let's get down to business. The letter. It deserves a response. I could 'produce' something and send it in an airtight container? Perhaps via 24-hour courier so it's still warm when it gets there? But Mr Tipple might be able to track it back to us. And besides, the package might leak. Or maybe I could send a one-word response? Something like "Arsewipe". (Technically two words, but the opportunity is too good to miss and I don't think he'd notice.) No. That's not courteous. It would be far better to draft a proper letter. A polite one, with subtle wording. We'll do that in a bit. Before we do, let's review the content of Mr Tipple's letter.

Among Mr Tipple's poor English and abusive comments is a valid point. We traditional anglers *are* an odd bunch, insofar as we're different to 'normal' folk (who apparently couldn't give a fig about what happened yesterday). I share his acknowledgement that the past is gone. However, he's wrong about us wanting to live in the past (if we did, we might never have experienced some of the greatest inventions in history, such as the electric guitar and the drawstring Wonderbra). Also, he's misinformed if he thinks that celebrating tradition is a waste of time. The past informs the present. Honouring it gives us a safer passage into the future.

C.S. Lewis wrote, "The future is something which everyone reaches at the rate of sixty minutes an hour, whatever he does, whoever he is". Good point. It makes us want to leave our watches in a drawer for a while, doesn't it? Especially when we read T.S. Eliot's words that "there is only ever time present". Seems like we're on *The Final Destination Express*, moving steadily along, throwing our past out of the window like well-chewed gum that's lost its flavour. Face facts: the past *is* lost, and the future has yet to be found. (One could argue that it's the other way round: that the future is lost and much of the past has yet to be discovered. But that's a different debate.)

The present is such a fleeting event, a microsecond between the past and the future, so short as to barely exist. Some will say that we must celebrate the moment, cherish the now, and become part of the time in which we live. This isn't, however, an excuse to abandon or forget the past. Our collective experiences educate us; our personalities are the result of a lifetime of living, thinking, and dreaming. The past, you could say, defines us.

"Doin whatyou do." These were interesting words in Mr Tipple's letter. If my translation of his scrawl is accurate, he was onto something there. "Doing what we do" is a sort of "Cogito ergo sum" (I think therefore I am). Yes, I like that. It's what I call a Descartes moment. "How do you do?" someone might ask; and a very English question it would be, too. But do we stop to think what 'doing' involves? It doesn't just refer to our wellbeing; it's a holistic question requiring a general answer. "How d'you do?" they ask. We pause and think about the activities that give us purpose, that define us, that enable 'you' to exist. "Very well, thank you," we might reply. "I wrote ten letters today, weeded the vegetable patch, went fishing, and spent quality time with my family; all before teatime." They're activities that, for the fleeting second, were our present – but very quickly becoming our past. A past that, although gone, defines us.

Connecting with the past provides us with a sense of heritage, provenance and history. It adds value to vintage things. Especially when it comes to traditionally-styled attire, such as English brogues, where we get a feeling of 'stepping into' history.

It was my friend Phinehas Foley who introduced me to the concept of 'traditions kept alive by those who wear them'. I remember asking Phin' why he switched from a trendy city life working in the music business (he was a songwriter) to taking it easy in the countryside wearing traditional tweed, smoking a clay pipe and writing poetry with a vintage fountain pen. "Fennel," he replied, "when reeling from a former life, you find yourself travelling backwards. I chose to look in this retrospective direction and found it so very interesting. These days I get all my inspiration from the past, where I seek to understand the values, customs and fashions of an earlier age. You gotta look backwards to go forwards."

Valuable advice from Phinehas, which just about concludes our discussion. Now the fun bit. The response to Mr Tipple. Let's start by getting his name right, then give him the consideration he deserves:

Dear Mr Nipple

I acknowledge receipt of your undated letter which highlights the importance of time. In it you provide educated opinion as to the perspective needed for people fishing in this current day and age. I agree with your comment that there is no point in attempting to live in the past. It is gone; along it seems with the ability to add punctuation when scratching the page with a Biro. But I am touched that you put your thoughts onto paper and sent them to me. However, given that they were sent second-class, I find them a little dated. One needs to stay focused on today. I trust you understand why this prevents me from continuing our correspondence.

Yours,

Fennel

P.S.

Ruled paper is so nice, isn't it? Having a reference line to guide your hand from side to side must have helped immensely given that it's likely to be the opposite direction to which it normally travels.

Yep. That ought to do it. He should now understand that we traditionalists live only for the present, and don't stand for any messing.

Ooh. Hang on. What's that? An uprising? Pass me my musket old chum, I think there's a Roundhead at the door!

XVI

PIKE!

Greetings from the fast lane of traditional angling. I am sitting in my car, racing into a fully embraced future. I'm driving rather too quickly, with one hand on the steering wheel and the other around this pen, trying to get home after being away for too long.

Earlier today I was en route to a date with a feisty female, who each winter makes me stand outside for ours in the freezing cold with no guarantee that she will respond to my advances. I just stand, and watch, and wait. I keep plugging away, hoping for a quick snap tackle. But it's more likely that I will receive her usual indifference and end up being the lonely sprat, bunged out in the cold. With all her coldness I still enjoy winding her up, hoping to tempt her rage and get her to bite. She likes it that way. I imagine her lying there, her eyes gazing up at me and her long slender body writhing and trembling as she readies herself...for the kill. I'm talking, of course, about a pike.

When referring to this freshwater predator, one should utter its name with the same alarming shriek as a swimmer announcing the presence of a shark.

I say again, "Pike!" A pitiless killer, ferocious and savage, a pike waits, lurks, and then attacks without mercy. It lunges with chilling intent. It's a cold-blooded murderer; a bringer of death. Just the challenge I needed following the recent 'dispatch'.

I'm not normally confrontational. In fact I'm rather cowardly when it comes to bar-room brawls and playground scrapes, but I feel quite butch and red-blooded when fishing for pike. It's not a feeling I often get (except when shopping for socks at Marks & Spencer, when I remain focused and forthright and not at all distracted by the posters of 'advertised wears' in the nearby lingerie section). So I have to admit to a sudden surge of testosterone this morning as I drove to the river. I was screaming aloud to Led Zeppelin's *Immigrant Song*, which pounded loudly from my car stereo; my head was rocking forward and back to the music and, while I convinced myself that my head-banging years were not over, a passer-by would have thought I was riding a miniature rocking horse in the car. It mattered not. I knew that very soon the hunter would become the hunted and that there would be a new daddy at the top of the food chain.

The only downside to pike fishing is that it's best done in winter. Whilst we might romanticise about the thought of hoar frost on bare branches and cat ice forming at the water's edge, fishing in such conditions is like leaning over and kissing the inside of a chest freezer. You do it once and, although awkward, find yourself stuck there for some considerable time.

Today is especially cold. I admit to having had second thoughts about fishing, but I started the day by reading Eric Marshall-Hardy's *Angling Ways*. Published in 1934, it must have been a welcome release from the struggles of the recent Great Depression. If people then could fish after such hardship then I could endure some minor toe numbing for my troubles. I would brave the cold and go spinning for pike. As Marshall-Hardy instructed, "Spinning is admitted to be the most sporting and skilful means of catching pike...I doubt if there is a subject in the realms of angling more interesting, complicated and open to varying opinion that that of pike spinning lures".

Exciting stuff, eh? No wonder I skipped breakfast in favour of rummaging through my fishing shed. I found the required items: a Scottie salmon spinning rod; an Altex reel; some wire trace; and a box of plugs, spinners and spoons. With my Sherlock Holmes deerstalker pulled tightly onto my head and tied firmly under my chin, my scarf wrapped high around my ears, and a grimace pinned to my face, I loaded the car and set forth to the river. That was five hours ago. Things didn't exactly go to plan.

I arrived at the Thames at 10.30am to find it looking lifeless and with no more call to action than a sign saying "Brown". I continued driving, thinking that I could always fish a lake. But conditions were worsening. An icy wind was blasting from the east and there was sleet in the air. *Maybe I could find a sheltered spot? Somewhere to sit it out before the fishing begins?* And then a location presented itself. I was driving along by the river at Lechlade when I spied a pub. A rather nice and traditional-looking pub. A pub called The Trout.

To set the record straight, and in case Mrs H ever reads this, I will say, quite adamantly, that my intentions today were to spin for pike. I absolutely wanted to stand in the cold, with my feet and hands freezing, wiping clear the drips that formed on my nose. I wanted to be chilled to the point where my limbs might snap off, and I definitely wanted to record the exact temperature at which my eyeballs froze over. The fact that my car had other plans was entirely beyond my control.

As I drove towards the pub, I felt the steering wheel swerve as the car swung sharply into the pub car park. The driver's door flung open and the car kicked me out. As I tumbled onto the ground, I heard the car shouting its orders at me to get it a pint of petrol and a packet of wheel nuts. It's not my fault that the pub didn't sell these. Don't blame me that the barman invited me to sample the cask ale and try one of his freshly made steak and kidney pies. Don't accuse me of weakness if you learn that I was forced to eat a dessert. And don't suggest that just because the pub dated back to 1220 AD, had elm beams, oak panels and stone floors, cased fish on its walls, and controlled two miles of fishing on the river, that I was inclined to stay longer than was *absolutely* necessary. As I said earlier, I was in a butch frame of mind, so these things were of no interest to me. Whatever happened at the pub was merely a temporary distraction. I was only interested in fishing. Only desiring to catch a pike. Only wanting to haul a fish from the water and feel the thrusting, pumping, pounding might of an ego satisfied by victory.

So why did I stay there for five hours? As you've probably guessed, that was the 'absolutely necessary' time to spend in such a wonderful place. But in winter, when I'm about as butch as a Chihuahua in a Tutu and as thrusting as a donkey on a pogo stick, I could easily have stayed longer. But I wasn't wearing a tutu. I was wearing two sets of long johns and had a hot water bottle sloshing about in my undies. So, without a valid excuse, I decided to stay there, drooling at the thought of a crusty puff topping. And pies being what they are, when served with ale, it only seemed right to finish off the meal by eating a sponge pudding with custard. I was feeling rather cosy, but then, just as I was about to leave, I endured a situation I'd rather have avoided.

I was just about to stand up and pay for my food when two large, bearded men walked into the snug. They were wearing chunky thermal wellingtons, all-in-one quilted suits and fleece hats with the word 'Esox' embroidered onto them. They each ordered a pint of super-strength lager and then sat down at the table opposite me. They had the look of real pike men. You know, the sort of adventurers who wrestle polar bears, drink whisky from the bottle and shave their heads with a Bowie knife. Tough men, forged from steel and as hard as granite. I looked at them and, in a moment of awkwardness, made eye contact with one of them for slightly too long. The hot water bottle nestling in my crotch went cold, my long johns started to itch and, as I felt my face start to tremble, I wished I'd removed my hat and scarf. I sank in my seat and looked away; keen to avoid further contact with these predator hunters. And then it happened.

"Hey, you!"

I kept my eyes focused on the custardy remains of my Spotted Dick.

"Didn't you used to be Fennel Hudson?"

Oh no, I would have to engage.

"No. You must be mistaken. My name's not Fennel." I replied.

"It *is* you! You're Fennel Hudson. You once fished in a celebrity pike match at Walthamstow reservoir. You fished with Chris Tarrant and Mick Brown. I remember!"

"Erm, maybe."

"That's right. You're the one who went out in that

crappy little dinghy in the howling wind and got blown out onto the island. You waved your arms about like a right wuss until someone noticed you. They had to call the lifeguard who rescued you in a speedboat. It ruined the fishing for everyone."

"Well, possibly."

"You came ashore looking like a kid who'd dropped his lolly into a puddle. You then sat in the clubhouse with a mug of tea for the rest of the day while us real anglers attempted to catch a pike."

"I've got over it now."

"I can see that. Landlord, a drink for our new friend. What'dya reckon Ted? Babycham, straight glass, with an umbrella?"

"Thanks guys."

"Ah, we're only messing with you. That gale was something else. Couldn't believe you attempted to go out in a boat. You did make us laugh though, wearing all those tweedy clothes and fishing with wooden rods. Who ever heard of such a thing? What did we call you? Oh, yes, that was it. The Walthamstow Woodentop. Watching you trying to cast a deadbait was hilarious, we weren't sure whether your knees or rods would go first, they were wobbling so much."

"It was the cold."

"Those long girlie socks weren't up to the job then?"

"They were sporting socks, worn with breeks."

"Ay, or a skirt."

"I've still got them."

"For wearing at the weekend, eh Shirley?"

"No, actually, they're my favourite attire."

"Oh, man. You're going to tell us you still use all that vintage gear, aren't you."

"Yup."

"Then there's no hope. You might as well stay in the pub. You'll never catch anything fishing like that, other than a cold that is. But then, there's no point going to the river anyway. We took one look at it and came straight here, glad to be wearing our long johns under all this clobber, *'cos it's bloomin' freezing out there.*"

The angler looked at me for a while and a smile appeared on his face. His shoulders relaxed and he let out a laugh. He'd been messing with me all along.

It seemed that we three anglers weren't that different, after all.

XVII

FROZEN

The weather is still bitterly cold. I've learned from recent experience that it's best to stay indoors, savouring the warmth of an open fire. Jack Frost might be dancing gaily outside but I shall remain in my study, unaffected by the chill. Sadly, I didn't always have this wisdom.

Back in 1991, or rather more specifically on *Wednesday 14th February 1991*, I was a sixteen year-old art student. It was Valentine's Day and, delicate young thing that I was, I hid in terror at the thought of spending a day surrounded by sexually-charged and 'curiously bumpy' creative girls who knew exactly what to do with a leek, an onion, and a wide bristled brush. It also happened to be Bernard Venables' birthday. So I feigned a stomach upset and stayed at home. At least until I hit on the idea of having my first-ever 'Crabtree Day' in honour of Bernard.

My Crabtree Day would involve fishing with my grandfather's tackle as usual, but with an extra dose of angling spirit. I would, as Mr Crabtree said, "See if we can't get as good fishing in winter as summer!" Given that carp were my regular summer fish, I would fish for them as opposed to the perch that I'd normally angle for in February. But I'd need to know more about how to catch carp in winter.

My usual approach to catching carp – floating breadcrust next to lily beds – would be unlikely to work at this bleak time of year. So I took a look though my family's library of fishing books and magazines. Eventually I found what I was looking for: an article entitled *The Key to Cold-weather Carp Fishing*. Written by the appropriately named Mike Winter (now a close friend of mine), it featured in the March 1965 edition of *Fishing* magazine. The feature described the methods suitable for catching carp in winter which, I was pleased to read, included using bread as bait. It was inspiring reading. My youthful enthusiasm overflowed and I found myself threading six-pound line through my grandfather's split cane Avon rod. And, adding to my excitement, ten inches of snow had fallen during the previous two days. Encouraged by the whiteout's ability to form an impassable snowdrift between me and the girls at college, I would be able to savour pure and *proper* winter fishing.

8.30am arrived, and with it departed the bus I would normally have caught to college. As it slipped and slid along the icy road, gritty ice-like snow fell from an orange-grey sky and I turned in the other direction towards my favourite carp lake.

I was wearing my warmest clothing, in fact two layers

of everything, including underpants. And I needed it, too. My steps were through knee-deep snow and the air was so cold that it made my eyes sting and my face itch. My fishing tackle – rod holdall, creel, rucksack, bait bucket, primus stove, jerrycan of water, a deck chair, two hot water bottles, and a hessian sack containing four loaves of bread – was strapped to my bicycle with belts and rope. I added a snow shovel for good measure; anticipating snow drifts in the narrow lanes near to home. I pulled my woolly hat down to my eyebrows, kept my head low, and ventured into the whiteness.

Unable to mount the bicycle because of the deep snow and the amount of tackle tied to its frame, I opted to walk alongside it, pushing it along and using it as a support as I crunched through the snow. I took a right turn next to a spider-shaped beech tree, then a left next to an enormous cedar, then a right at some crossroads before climbing the highest and steepest hill known to man. Pushing the bike up this slope required me to kick my feet crampon-style into the snow and heave the bike a foot at a time, barely seeing the wheels turn with each lunge. I poised at the top of the hill and surveyed the winterscape. I could see my house a mile-and-a-half away, but not any further. Snow was falling in the distance creating a wall of white that would soon reach me. And before it, everything was eerily white. And silent. There were no cars, or animals in the fields, or birds in the sky. I was the only one brave enough to venture out. And as I looked back down the hill, I could barely see my footsteps in the snow. Was I here at all? Was I really going fishing in this? My pounding heart confirmed my presence, and my adrenaline told me I was going fishing. I was committed to the cause, determined to celebrate Bernard's birthday, and encouraged onwards by the words of an authority whose article had convinced me to fish for carp in winter.

I checked my pocket watch. 10.17am. Either the workings of the watch had slowed, or my journey had already taken me nearly two hours. I wasn't dismayed. To the west I could see the wood that surrounded the lake. It was only half a mile away. And all downhill. I could be there in twenty minutes. I set off like a tobogganist down the slope, sliding and careering through the snow, running in places as if trying to evade an avalanche.

Eventually I was in the wood, with the lake only a hundred yards away. The air was unnervingly quiet. The lack of birdsong seemed unnatural to my ears. But I convinced myself that soon I'd hear the clucking of moorhens and quacking of mallards. Perhaps even the crashing of a carp as it leapt clear of the water and landed with a loud "kersploosh"?

When I arrived at the lake, the image before me made me laugh out loud. There was no lake. No moorhens. No mallards. And no carp. Only an expanse of snow.

I laughed, and laughed, and laughed. I shook my

head, and then laughed some more. The snow that lay where the lake should be was at least two feet deep. The water beneath must have been frozen for days or weeks. If the carp were feeding, it was in the shadowy water beneath the ice and snow. I could see them no better than I could see common sense. Blinded by enthusiasm, I should have known that the lake would be frozen. The air temperature had barely risen above zero since Christmas. This was the coldest winter in years. But I could still break the ice, right?

I cleared away the snow from the ground around my feet, found a rock the size of a house brick, kicked it free from the frozen soil, picked it up, juggled it in my hand, and then threw it out into the expanse of snow. It landed with a soft thud. There was no cracking or shattering of ice. Just the rock sitting there, staring back at me with an unreserved look that said but one word: "Fool".

Normally, in situations like this, I'd sit back and make a cup of tea. But I couldn't even do that. The water in my jerrycan had frozen.

And then the realisation: what if someone was watching me? Would they be raising an eyebrow at my novice antics? Would they be laughing at my hopelessness? Would they know, with the obviousness of what they saw before them, that I was no more able to fish than confront the girls at college? I couldn't bear the thoughts. So I did what any self-respecting, experienced and authoritative winter carp angler would do: I carried on as though nothing was amiss.

I stood beside the 'lake', glancing left to right as I made an informed survey of the likely feeding spots. And then I got to work. I removed all the gear from my bike. I unfolded the chair, tackled up my rod and net, pushed a bankstick into the snow, removed a loaf from the hessian bag, hooked a chunk of crust to the line, and then swung the bait out onto the snow, ten feet away. I then placed to rod in its rest and sat down, not taking my eyes off the bait that lay there like a disgruntled scrap rejected by the pigeons. I lurched forward towards the rod a few times, just in case anyone was watching, but then, ten minutes later, I reeled in, packed up and headed home.

My mother was waiting at the front door of our house when I got back. Her knowing smile said it all, but she made the comment anyway: "Frozen, was it?"

I went upstairs to my bedroom and confronted the article about winter carp fishing. I must have missed some crucial information because, during my ten minutes of fishing, the carp hadn't shown the slightest interest in my bait.

There, on the first page, written most clearly, was the caveat to the instruction. That carp could be caught in winter "under suitable conditions". 'Suitable', as I now realised, meant decidedly *unwinterlike* conditions. Those days that feel more like spring, or winters when the wind comes from the south and ice hardly forms. Not, as I had previously thought, during the most *extreme* winter conditions. Still, at least I'd ticked the 'expert' box. I'd become a pioneer: of snow fishing for carp. All I had to do was write about it, and my efforts would be explained...

Stop – Unplug – Escape – Enjoy

What type of angling, in what
conditions, would you most
like to pioneer?

XVIII

A REEL FOR CHRISTMAS

It's nice to know that an angler's spirit can never truly be dampened. Whatever the weather or circumstance, there's always an opportunity to fish for something – even if it's just for laughs or ideas. Which is just what we need when others might seek to sanitise our way of living. Fortunately, some traditions continue regardless. Take Christmas for example: it's a day to celebrate a special birthday with a midnight mass and lighting of a candle, a time to give and receive presents while our homes are adorned with tinsel and holly, and a opportunity to slump in front of the television to watch a scantily-clad Ursula Andress appear from the ocean. Again.

Christmas is special. As a child, I yearned for the excitement and anticipation of giving and receiving presents; later in life I appreciated the importance of faith at this time of year, and now I enjoy all the above with the added 'bounce' of the 3.30pm well-filled bikini.

Which is what I'm currently anticipating. I'm slumped on the sofa, watching the television. James Bond is singing about mangoes and I'm about to sleep-off an enormously ambitious helping of roast potatoes. But before I do, I want to share with you the reasons why this Christmas is my best to date.

As I lie here on the settee, nursing my stomach and trying hopelessly to reach for my twenty-seventh *After Eight* mint, I am reminded of all the fine things I've received as presents over the years: a bendy-legged Godzilla; a Batman costume (when Batman wore grey leggings and a silk mask with rather surprised-looking eyebrows drawn onto it); an Action Man with moveable eyes; my first Barbour jacket; a bone-handled penknife; a pair of Brasher walking boots; BB's *Letters from Compton Deverell*; a Mabie Todd fountain pen; a box of Derwent pencils; a 1930s valve amp radio; a Barder *Carpcrawler* rod; a bottle of vintage port and a two-year-old 'sludge' of stilton (not for the delicate of stomach). Then there's this year's present. A present so special that it took Santa eighteen months to deliver it.

Mrs H has excelled herself with her present to me this year. As many wives know, buying a present for an angler-husband is fraught with difficulty. The spouse has to know exactly what her partner wants. Anglers are usually very precise in their tastes. It isn't good enough for them to ask Santa for "a fishing rod" or even "a trout fishing rod". Santa needs to know the length, action and maker if he's to get close to what is required. And in the case of vintage tackle as a present,

Santa needs a photo and detailed description, including year, condition, distinguishing marks, and whether the item has ever been within a hundred yards of water. If this information isn't provided, then the angler has to prepare himself for the worst. His Christmas could go something like this:

"Here you go, Darling. Your main present. You asked for a vintage basket to keep your tackle in when fishing, so I did some research and got you this."

Your heart pounds, your fingers tremble. Could it be the pot-bellied, leather-trimmed wicker creel you always dreamed about? Your family sits around you, watching in anticipation, waiting to see your response. You peel away the wrapping paper to reveal...a bright blue plastic seat box with foam-padded carry strap. You smile politely, thanking your beloved for such a thoughtful present, while secretly planning to flog the item before Boxing Day.

When it comes to vintage tackle, plastic just doesn't make the grade. Traditional angling is not a Tupperware Party for the overly sentimental. There's no airtight seal or cling film suffocating that which we love. Foam handles on rods? Injection-moulded rod rests and tackle boxes that shut with a 'clunk'? They are but crinkly bin liners reeking of unnatural production and chemical interference. (Quite similar, I would imagine, to the pong from Frankenstein's toilet.) As traditionalists, we know that mass-produced items are the plastic bib around the neck of a spoon-fed generation. We are different.

We want to touch and feel proper craftsmanship, smell the varnish of a new rod and hear birdsong when we fish (while ignoring the hypocrisy of using nylon fishing lines and having a mobile phone in our pocket).

Using traditional tackle is not the same as collecting it. I know that some vintage tackle enthusiasts keep their collections locked away behind glass doors. They wouldn't dream of exposing them to the elements or bringing them anywhere near a bucketful of fermenting bait. These people are more akin to museum curators than traditional anglers. They purchase rare pieces and keep hold of them as an investment, ultimately selling them when the market price provides an acceptable return. Gazing upon their collections is impressive, but it can be slightly nauseating when you're confronted with so much mint condition vintage tackle. These items haven't lived. They've been stuck in a cell and only hear about fish and watery places from the more battered items that are occasionally added to the collection. They have no memories of their own. They are like postage stamps that never went on a journey.

Of course, we need collectors to preserve our tackle heritage. But I am an angler, not a collector. I have no desire to own a reel that cost more than my car. Any items I have are to be used, and are by no means expensive collector's pieces. They will get scuffed and scraped, but with every mark comes another memory and story to tell. How else would our tackle gain sentimental value?

Users of vintage tackle are occasionally accused of recklessness. "How can he afford to fish with such tackle? What if it breaks?" But they will defend their actions by saying that they at least know what it feels like to use the tackle. Like those who would open a bottle of vintage wine, users of traditional tackle can say that they have experienced and savoured the product. They know what lies within.

Of course, there comes a time when all tackle should be retired from service and moved one step closer to the Cupboard of Rest. I fear the day when my favourite reel is held in my hand and I say, "Sorry old-timer, it's a tartan shawl and rubber underpants for you. You'll like it on the retirement shelf, though, it's got a nice view through the window and you won't be far from the Scrabble board. I'll look you up every now and then and bring you photos of the angling I've done with your younger, stronger and better-looking replacement. Just try not to dribble too much, and remember to put your teeth in before you eat a boiled egg". With luck, that day is far off for most of my tackle. Why? Because most of it isn't vintage at all, just vintage-styled reproductions made by skilled modern-day craftsmen. I have rods by Barder and reels by Hardy, J.W. Young and now, after a gap of six years, a centrepin made by the doyenne of reelmakers.

I can now reveal that my Christmas present is a Richard Carter twelve spoke aerial centrepin.

Not a second-hand one from an auction house but one made brand new, in secret, by its maker. Commissioned by my good lady after meeting Richard at a social event, it is the most perfect centrepin I've ever seen. Four-and-a-half inch diameter, with nickel silver fittings, tortoiseshell handles, antique effect finish and an agate 'eye' on the rear. It spins for nearly a minute and its ratchet ticks as sweetly as a Sturmey Archer hub on a freewheeling bicycle. "But Richard Carter retired eleven years ago!" I hear you cry. That's true, but he was lured out of retirement by Mrs H to make a special reel to signify my return to health. It's not a collectors' piece that's destined for a glass case. It's not a 'number one', or 'number two' or even 'number three' in a manufacturing run. It is a late model in the career of a great reelmaker, and possibly the last he'll ever sell. For Richard is most definitely retired and now has other commitments that keep him busy and away from his lathe.

After opening my present this morning, and picking myself up off the floor, I telephoned Richard, telling him how thrilled I was with the reel. His response of, "Oh, I'm glad you like it," summed up his modesty and slight embarrassment that I should be so vocal in singing his praises. But it was his closing comment that took me aback and got me thinking. He said, "I probably shouldn't tell you this but I nearly died making that reel for you. I was in my shed, dunking the reel into antiquing solution, when the gas that was fizzing from the mixture became too much to bear. I stumbled out of the shed, coughing and spluttering, my lungs burning and my head feeling like it was about to explode. I was ill for several days. It must have been something to do with the arsenic in the mix". Hearing this, I knew that the reel must always be used. With a story like that, it would be a crime to keep the reel locked away as an investment piece. Richard Carter, one of the greatest modern-day reel-makers, risked his life to make me this reel. While there are more collectable and expensive reels out there, none carry the story of the reel made for me, and could never make me feel the way I do now.

I have the Carter centrepin next to me as I write these words. It is more than an instrument with which to fish. As it spins, it represents what has passed and what will be. It is testament to my friendship with Richard, to traditional angling, and to the love of my wife who made me very happy on Christmas Day. With these words, I thank them most sincerely.

Stop – Unplug – Escape – Enjoy

What fishing-related thing would
you most like as a present?

XIX

THE EDWARD BARDER INTERVIEW

Edward Barder is one of the most respected makers of split cane fishing rods in the world. He's also a friend of mine. So I thought I'd tell you a little bit about him, and then pop along to his workshop to discuss the magic that goes into making his rods.

Edward rose to prominence in 1992 when Chris Yates – the UK's leading traditional angler – wrote about his rods in the book *The Secret Carp*. These rods, like the book, have since become modern-day classics. The Barbus Maximus, Carpcrawler, Bishop, and Merlin were described with affection and praise. It was enough for me to prise open my piggy bank and start counting my pennies.

Three years later, and after a fortuitous serious of events, I was standing next to Edward and Chris at the AGM of the Golden Scale Club. We began speaking about rods and I was immediately impressed by Edward's passion and knowledge of the best bamboo rods of the last 100 years. Chris remarked about Edward's unfaltering attention to detail and suggested that Edward and I should meet up to discuss rods for my carp and barbel fishing. Edward and I agreed to meet one week later.

The day came, and I cycled from my cottage at Lambourn to Edward's workshop in Newbury. Edward put the kettle on and we talked about my requirements. The result was that I ordered a Barbus Maximus rod – an 11ft 9in two-piece rod with detachable handle. I was so impressed with Edward's skills that I also entrusted my grandfather's cane rod with him to restore.

Eighteen months later and my rods were complete. The Barbus Maximus was superb and my grandfather's rod (an R. Sealey's Precise) was presented in better condition than when it was new. As a result, Edward and I began a special relationship where I trust him implicitly to deliver on his reputation for making the best split cane rods available.

Edward has earned his reputation. When someone purchases a rod from him, he or she is not just buying bamboo, cork and metal; they're buying a lifetime's research and experience. Hence why I recommend Edward as my rodmaker of choice. But Edward's rods are not cheap. Some people may baulk at paying nearly two thousand pounds for a fishing rod. But consider: if you wrote to a world-class craftsman and asked them to make something just for you, how much money would you table to get their attention?

At 2010 prices, a bait-fishing rod from Edward will cost you in excess of £1,200 and a three-piece (spare tip) fly rod will cost £1,900. That amount of money could buy a great many second-hand cane rods or new rods by lesser makers. But that's not the point. If you want the best, you might as well buy from the best. (No point wasting all your life searching car boot sales for a Barder rod or Purdey shotgun. You might as well make your investment and watch it appreciate in value.) And the price is not extortionate when you consider the work that's gone into it. A split cane bamboo rod takes sixty hours or more to build. The result is a bamboo rod of unsurpassed quality, that's more than a fishing tool. It is a totem, a declaration of our identity as a traditional angler and as a connoisseur of bamboo rods. It's also a statement that we believe in the need to be different, and that we've earned the right to treat ourselves to something special.

Point made? I hope so. Time to mount our bicycles and pay Edward a visit.

The Edward Barder Rod Company, Newbury, Berkshire.

Edward Barder's workshop on the banks of the river Lambourn in Berkshire has barely changed in twenty years. It's little more than a lean-to shed, albeit one dignified by age and its proximity next to a beautiful period building. But it's the magic that goes on inside the workshop that makes it so inviting.

The greeting I always receive from Edward and his colleague Colin, of "Fancy a cuppa?" has a family-like warmness. (I always take biscuits with me, knowing that Edward and Colin are as excited by the prospect of tea and biscuits as I am of discussing rods.) Add to this Edward's aura of authority, humility and dry sense of humour, and I'm immediately put at ease. After a brew and a packet of biscuits, we're ready to talk about rods.

Fennel: To begin with, what's your opinion of modern split cane rod-making?

Edward: There are more people making the right kind of effort these days than fifteen-or-so years ago. In the early nineties, when I set up The Edward Barder Rod Company, there were split cane rodmakers in existence because of the growing enthusiasm for split cane rods. They were on the bandwagon, part of the acolyte fever for Chris Yates, selling rods but bypassing the usual rod making apprenticeship.

Fennel: Did that affect the quality of their rods?

Edward: The quality of the split cane rods made in the UK in the nineties, and to some degree today, was representative of the cottage industry of split cane rodmaking. It's an easy market to get into, with small start-up costs. A few known tapers, a shed in the garden, a website, maybe even a testimonial or two in the press, and they're in business.

Fennel: Easy to get into but difficult to endure?

Edward: The split cane rod making industry isn't

regulated like it is for gun makers, where all guns have to pass quality testing. Split cane rods can be sold without any stamp of approval. However, split cane rodmakers today are competing in a limited market. They are selling to the same customers who tend to demand quality. If it's not there, the rodmaker doesn't survive.

Fennel: The industry sounds tough. Can you explain?

Edward: Cane rods are not mainstream and therefore appeal to a minority. Would-be rodmakers should acknowledge the demanding quality expectations of the split cane connoisseur. The romantic charm of the split cane 'cottage' industry may sound appealing, especially after reading a book (usually the one by Garrison and Carmichael) or being encouraged by friends. But it is like any other business. Competition prevails.

Fennel: Turning one's hobby into a business is a challenge in itself.

Edward: New rodmakers might have other sources of income, have free time, be genuinely skilled, or have a pressing ambition to make cane rods. However, reality soon kicks in if quality or efficiency is lacking. The rodmaker must deliver the required volume and quality of rods if they are to consistently delight their customers – and make ends meet. The industry is better because of this, and the customer now has greater reassurance that their money will be well invested.

Fennel: Even though split cane rods built today are five times more expensive than those made in the nineties?

Edward: Split cane rods are getting better and better. Many rodmakers today have done more than read a book; they have studied their craft and inspected the rods made in years gone by. Rod making generates small profits, which may be okay for a hobby business, but provides limited luxuries for those making rods full-time.

Fennel: How would you make an economical success at making rods?

Edward: I'm still searching for the answer to that question! What is essential, though, is that the rodmaker persistently drives to improve their skill, and the quality of their rods, whilst remaining realistic about the economics of their venture.

Fennel: I notice your milling machine. Does this give you economic advantages over hand-planing?

Edward: Planing by hand doesn't usually allow a commercial rodmaker to make enough rods to make a living. Also, it would be a long time before the rodmaker completed enough rods to know and learn his craft. That said, Homer Jennings uses a hand plane. He's successfully done so for thirty years or more. His fastidiousness, experience and skill as an angler have ensured that this approach has worked.

Fennel: So it's the knowledge and skill of the rodmaker that makes the difference, rather than the equipment?

Edward: A rodmaker should be steeped in the historical aspects of rod making. How can you have confidence in your quality if you don't know the best rods of the past and present?

Fennel: How did you go about learning this?

Edward: I made it my business to understand what makes excellent, highest quality tackle. I worked in the tackle trade – at Hardy's – to appreciate the workmanship in the best quality split cane rods: what they should and shouldn't do. I talked to old rodmakers and their contemporaries; I wrote to every notable US rodmaker, read every US and UK book and article on rod making that I could find; I went to every tackle auction I could until I'd seen all the best rods. I studied hard until I knew the standards that had to be achieved. Only then did I do my own thing.

Fennel: That gave you the knowledge to begin, but what about now?

Edward: Even with all that knowledge, I never stopped actively learning. Being well informed of what is good was okay when I started, but not now. Today you have to focus on the minutiae of detail if you aspire to be the best. A single air bubble in the varnish is enough to reject a rod. Today the market is demanding, with global competition. Everything has to be as near to perfect as possible.

Fennel: Given the global scale of the bamboo rod market, who would you list as your contemporaries?

Edward: Homer Jennings; Per Brandin; Mark Aroner (who worked for Leonard and for Thomas

& Thomas); Walt Carpenter (who worked for Paine); Winston and Orvis have made a great many good rods; The interconnected Denver firms of Wright and McGill (who developed the Eagle Claw hook), Goodwin Granger and Phillipson produced rods in considerable volume and to very high standards; Pezon et Michel made very good cane rods – which now go for big money as buyers are realising how good the rods are.

Fennel: What would be the next step to learning the rodmaker's trade?

Edward: Once the required quality is known, the rodmaker needs to understand the fundamentals of rod building (how to select the best raw materials and how to use them to the best effect), and know that preparation and final manufacture need to be absolutely refined. Tolerances worked to for a structurally sound rod should be applied to all rods, not just cane.

Fennel: For split cane rods, what specifically needs to be addressed?

Edward: Split cane rods have to be really accurately made. They must be a proper hexagon, made from perfect triangles. With cane there shouldn't be any aspect of the rod in question. It should be the greatest perfection that hand and mind can create.

Fennel: What do you think caused the obsessive quality in bamboo rods?

Edward: In the 1980s and early '90s there was a coming together of very keen fly fishermen who had read the Garrison and Carmichael book. They were influenced by the book in every area; all worked to near-impossible standards. These became the mythical 'American Standards', which spread to the rest of the world. America was then, and still is, the stronghold of bamboo rod making.

Fennel: You're doing a very good job flying the British flag among rodmakers worldwide. What's your secret?

Edward: The 'Edward and Colin' ethos is, "Do it as well as it can be done or don't do it at all". Never, ever, will we accept a 'that will do' mentality. We now have the workshop equipped to make every part of the rod except for the rings. This ensures we keep control of the production quality, enabling consistent and repeatable results via practised hand skills. It's a trusted system; time consuming, yes, but the enjoyment we and our customers get from the results makes it worthwhile.

Fennel: Does the would-be rodmaker have a lot of catching up to do to achieve world-class standards?

Edward: The chances of reaching the highest standards are, for most people, slim. The rodmaker has to be a genuinely good craftsman, be patient, methodical, have a good eye, enjoy fishing, use a system (e.g. Garrison) and make rods to known measurements and deploy all their skills and meticulousness. If they are honest and really challenge their results – with rigidly high standards – they 'could' make terrific rods. With a particular comfort zone or type of fishing rod, the maker could potentially be a new breed of maker. But they would have to be very gifted and determined to succeed.

Fennel: How would this translate into advice for the would-be rodmaker?

Edward: Don't fool yourself that you know more than you do. The benchmark is high, so work your apprenticeship.

Fennel: Tell me about tapers.

Edward: Tapers have to be carefully thought out and precisely adhered to, especially with today's specialised uses that require faster tapers. A rod's action is principally the result of the taper, which must be harmonious between one section and the other and match the type of fishing that the rod is designed for. A bamboo rod is superior to other materials – for the type of fishing it's designed for – and vice-versa. Take the Peter Stone 'Legerstrike' for example; it's a heavy tool with eighteen inches of fine tip. The fibreglass version got away with the radical taper, but the cane version suffers from a dog-leg where the thin cane quickly joins thicker cane.

Fennel: Most of your rods utilise your own tapers, which are now tried and tested. Can you tell me about them?

Edward: Designing my own tapers was initially a matter of trial and error. But Colin and I have fished all our lives and so were able to assess the rods in use and put them through their paces. With experience, I knew just what changes needed to be made so that the rod performed exactly as I'd intended. These days I have specialised computer software, based on maths provided by Garrison, that enables me to understand to some extent how a rod will flex even before it's built. If I have any doubts then my network of rod-building friends is there to validate the tapers. But cane is a natural material. A computer-designed taper doesn't accommodate all of the variables involved. The tempering of bamboo, for example, is crucial. If too blonde and soft, or too burnt and brittle, the rod will behave differently to the intended action. Getting this right is a matter of experience.

Fennel: For some buyers, it's the aesthetic beauty of bamboo that appeals.

Edward: People like the classic form, it gives reassurance that a design is trusted and accepted. Think of Purdey shotguns or Regency-styled buildings. They can be made new, using refined skills, whilst still maintaining the beauty of the original. Split cane rodmaking may be 100 years old, but modern bamboo rods are built using a sensitive balance of modern technology and craftsman skills.

Fennel: What's your criteria for selecting a cane rod?

Edward: There are six things:

1. Many people buy blind. I do not recommend this. The customer needs to either be so confident in the rodmaker's reputation, or they should go and see the maker and inspect the rods.

2. Know what you want the rod to do. With cane, the joy is in casting to and playing a fish. While you can take vitamin pills for nutrition, eating delicious fruit and veg is more enjoyable. It's the same with cane. But if you want something that can cast super-long distances or handle really heavy leads, then carbon is the better choice.

3. Keep emotion in the bag. Some potential customers are so wrapped up in the emotional appeal of cane that they overlook the functional requirements, especially with second-hand cane rods where one can never know their full history or if they've been overstrained.

4. The rod must stand up to scrutiny. Make sure you know what to look for. Check its build quality. Cast with it (if it's a fly rod); put a reel on it and check for balance, thread line through its rings and pull against a static object. Is the cane sound? Are the sections delaminating? Do the ferrules shake? Is the varnish sound? (On a rod 40 years old or more, the varnish will very probably be porous even if the rod's never been used. A varnish overcoat may be needed.)

5. If you can't inspect the rod, ensure the seller offers a returns policy, e.g. return the rod within ten days if not fully satisfied, and receive a full refund including postage costs.

6. The exception to these rules is if the rod is at a price where you can 'take a punt' and afford to lose money on it.

Fennel: Thank you Edward. Now, about that fly rod I intend to order...

While talking to Edward I became aware that his focus on excellence surpasses the mere aesthetics that attract many anglers to purchase and use bamboo rods. Whereas I'm a sucker for first impressions, and often make an emotional purchase, Edward's emphasis is on creating a rod that will do the job perfectly for which it is designed. He's a practical and logical man, a perfectionist and gifted craftsman. His rods are based upon twenty years' rodmaking experience and a lifetime of research. He's also an impressively skilled angler (he once held the River Kennet barbel record), so he can translate the needs of an angler into the design of his rods. And therein lies his genius.

Edward Barder understands what is needed, and has perfected what is possible. And judging by what he's achieved to date, I'd say he's setting the benchmark for cane users and rodmakers alike.

Stop – Unplug – Escape – Enjoy

If you were to design an item
of traditional fishing tackle, what
would it be and for what purpose
would it it be used?

XX

THE LAST CAST

As an angler-writer I'm entitled to one last cast, a final attempt to capture what I seek to convey. For this book about Traditional Angling, I can do no better than to quote directly from my 1998 angling diary:

I am fishing at my favourite carp pool. It is a timeless place, steeped in history and with atmosphere that forms in layers, much like the leaves that settle beneath the lakeside trees. This special place, this magical pool, has a tendency to affect my thoughts. Sometimes these thoughts are demonic; other times angelic. I've experienced both today: from an urge to hunt down the largest fish in the lake by using self-hooking rigs, super-strength carbon rods and PVA bags (all the things that 'dissolve' the spirit of angling), to reeling in and gazing up into the trees while listening to the birdsong and savouring the tranquillity of nothingness. How can two extremes be experienced on the same day? Is it the lake messing with my mind, or my mind trying to fathom the mysteries of this ancient place? My conclusion is that the spiritual side of angling kindles emotions that my mind foolishly tries to ponder. Such messages are for the heart, not the head. Intellect is wasted on such signals. Only emotion can decipher them.

"You want? You like?" The lake taunts me with glimpses of things I want to touch. I am weak. I answer: "Yes. Yes." But it is not my chosen path. I am here for reasons other than the great carp that inhabit this lake. I am a humble man, who fishes simply, with bamboo rod and basic baits. I dress in tweed and take pleasure in taking my time. I begin when I am ready. That is how it is. How I like it. I shun the lake's playful gestures and banish the demons within. A big fish, or the pursuit of any fish at the expense of savouring the day, is not for me. I wish for a simple life, with angling at its heart. For this, angling must also be simple. Perhaps how it once was. Perhaps how it will be again.

I write these words to cement my beliefs. Angling should be simple and pure. No corruption or urgency; no demons taunting us to take what should only ever be given. People will say I'm traditional, and that my angling is also traditional. It's not. I'm merely doing my own thing, following my instincts, 'angling' for whatever gentle pleasures I can find. Fish are the smallest yet most easily found piece of the jigsaw. With such puzzles I like to start in the middle and reach out to find the edges.

These words make sense to me, but they are only jottings in a diary. Others may not think as I do?

Who knows? Maybe one day someone will read these words and understand their meaning? Maybe they'll agree that catching a fish is the least important part of a successful day's angling. In fact, if I were to write a book about traditional angling, I'd make sure it didn't describe the capture of a single fish at all. I'd then wait until the end to see if anyone had noticed...

ABOUT THE AUTHOR

FENNEL HUDSON

*"Author, artist, naturalist and countryman. His is a
lifestyle to inspire the most bricked-up townie."*

Fennel Hudson is a lifestyle and countryside
author known for his *Fennel's Journal* books and
Contented Countryman podcasts. A member of the
Golden Scale Club, he was mentored from a young
age by famous angling-authors Chris Yates and
Bernard Venables. They taught him the importance of
sporting ethics and seasonality, and encouraged him to
view the natural world through artist's eyes. As someone
who seeks escapism through fishing, he's principally a
pleasure fisherman who uses bamboo rods and vintage
reels as a way of connecting with the timelessness of
the natural world. This gives him a unique perspective
of the true beauty (and humour) of angling, which he
shares in his message: 'Stop – Unplug – Escape – Enjoy'.

For more information please visit:
www.fennelspriory.com

THE FENNEL'S JOURNAL SERIES

THE FIRST-EVER REVIEWS OF FENNEL'S JOURNAL:

"Fennel's Journal began as a series of illustrated letters to friends. As these evolved they became less a diary, more a manifesto, and the Journal is now exactly that – a way of living, rurally and simply: very real for all those who recognise the importance of tradition and joy."

Caught by the River

"I can see where it might lead. What he has would make amazing TV. It's the Good Life, but in a realistic way. It's Jack Hargreaves. It's Countryfile. It's quality Sunday newspaper stuff. It's 1948, all over again. In trying to escape the present he's inevitably created a brand. A potentially very powerful brand."

Bob Roberts Online

"Fennel's Journal is a masterpiece about rural living. It is a route-map to the life we all seek."

The Traditional Fisherman's Forum

From A Meaningful Life:

"Life is the most beautiful and rewarding gift. We just need to take time out to allow us to reflect, change perspective, and see things in their best light. Sometimes we just have to stop and feel the pulse of the Earth, the rhythm of the seasons and the internal voice that was once our childhood friend. As the natural world grows smaller, so too does its intensity and the size of the window through which it may be viewed."

NO.1

A MEANINGFUL LIFE

A Meaningful Life is the first and perhaps most important Journal. It documents the origins of Fennel's Priory and why Fennel decided to live by a new set of ideals. With themes ranging from escapism, adventure, work-life balance, identity and purpose, through to traditionalism and country living, it sets the scene for future editions – building messages that are central to Fennel's Priory. Ultimately it conveys the importance of a relaxed, balanced, and meaningful life.

READER TESTIMONIALS

"I loved reading this Journal. It's inspiring and has the beginnings of something very special."

"Fennel's chosen trajectory is firmly in the slow lane. He's a countryman, with courage to stand behind his traditional values."

"Witty and emotive, Fennel's writing conveys passion for a slower-paced and quieter life."

From A Waterside Year:

"Water is intrinsically linked to the
mystery and excitement of discovering
new worlds. Of dreams. And hopes.
And thoughts of what 'could be'.
Dreams free us from normality.
...As the daydreams grew longer, the
distinction between what was real and
what was imaginary grew less. Soon I
existed in a blissful world of my own
creation. Reality, as I learned, is only a
matter of perception...A life that is real
to one is surreal to another."

NO. 2

A WATERSIDE YEAR

In *A Waterside Year*, Fennel takes time out to live beside
a lake in rural England. Here he appreciates the healing
qualities of water, studies the wildlife around him, lives
at the pace of someone outside of normal daily life, and
discovers the freedom that's found in isolation. Getting
so close to Nature, and generally spending time in idle
fashion, enables him to discover a stronger sense of self.
Ultimately he learns that freedom is not a place, but
something that exists within us.

READER TESTIMONIALS

*"A year in the wild. How we would all love to follow in
Fennel's stead and indulge our dreams, to come out the
other side a stronger and wiser person."*

*"A Journal with a message – that we should take time
out to think about what's important, and see the
beauty of the world."*

*"A truly blissful read full of inspiration and humour.
The story of Fennel sitting in his tent, with the noises
outside, had me laughing out loud!"*

From A Writer's Year:

"What I am interested in, what I write
and care about, exists in the slow lane,
somewhere between hand-ploughed
fields and a pint of real ale.
Writing, with a fountain pen and ink
from a bottle, onto real paper, is the
simplest of things. Yet it can transport
us to a different place entirely.
Imagination is the real magic that
exists in this world. Look inwards,
to see outwards. And capture it
in writing."

NO. 3

A WRITER'S YEAR

A Writer's Year celebrates the writer's craft. It champions the handwritten letter, discusses vintage pens and writing ink, and celebrates things such as antique typewriters and the quirkiness of the creative mind. It's a blend of observations. It's funny. It's serious. It's real life. But most of all it is written to encourage would-be writers to find their voice, to put pen to paper, and follow their dreams.

READER TESTIMONIALS

"What Fennel has written is not so much a eulogy for the handwritten letter as a call-to-arms for everyone to follow their dreams and make the most of their God-given talents. This is a genuinely inspiring read."

"It filled me with calm and smiles. I loved the part: 'If a pen can communicate our thoughts, dreams and emotions and be the voice of our soul, then ink is the medium that carries the message'. It shows how important and generous writing can be."

From Wild Carp:

"Some will say that searching for your dreams is like looking for unicorns in an emerald forest. They will say that following a golden thread will lead only to a king, dethroned and living in the gutter. This may be so.
But the king was made, not born.
The crown was never his to wear.
...If ever the adventure proves tiring, or you lose sight of your dream, look to the west at sunset. There, on days when the skies are clear, you might see upon the horizon a thin layer of golden mist. When it appears, you will know its purpose: it is the mist of believing."

WILD CARP

Angling for wild carp is about adventure, history, atmosphere and emotion. *Wild Carp* captures this aplenty, describing Fennel's 20-year quest to find a very special type of fish. But it's also about nature connection and a desire to uncover the seemingly impossible – a place where we can discover and live out our dreams, to completely indulge the mantra of 'Stop – Unplug – Escape – Enjoy'.

READER TESTIMONIALS

"When written well, traditional angling writing by the likes of BB, for example, is the type of literature that I can read again and again. Fennel's writing flows un-hurried without overly romanticising each point and the research is thorough; from the first sentence I was thinking, 'this lad can write!' It's informative and very refreshing."

"Such inspiring writing. His words 'Somewhere in the undergrowth of the impossible' had me staring out from the page in amazement. Fennel's writing is pure poetry."

From Fly Fishing:

"The deeper we travel into the natural
world, and the greater the number
of technological encumbrances we
leave behind, the more likely we are
to escape the fast-paced lifestyle and
stresses of the 21st Century.
For some, angling enables a quest
into the unknown, an adventure into
the wild. For these fortunate folk,
fly-fishing is escapism. Their hours
by water serve as contemplation to
enrich their souls, directing their quest
inwards, towards their longed-for
state of completeness."

NO. 5

FLY FISHING

Fly Fishing celebrates the most graceful and artful form of angling, explaining what it means to be an angler – in the spirit of Izaak Walton – and how fly fishers differ from bait fishers. The sporting and aesthetic beauty of fly-fishing is described in Fennel's usual witty and contemplative style. As he says, "Fly fishing is the ultimate form of angling; it gives us a reason to fish simply, travel lightly, and explore the wild places that replenish our soul. With a fly rod, we're not casting to a fish; rather to a circle of dreams: ripples that spread into every aspect of our lives".

READER TESTIMONIALS

"Brilliant writing. Fennel made me laugh out loud in bed. My wife was asking questions!"

"A delightful, well-articulated, read. I strongly recommend it, especially to the contemplative, tradition-loving, bamboo fly rod devotees among us."

"A very inspiring and rewarding read. I will try to tie the Sedgetastic fly. It looks tasty!"

From Traditional Angling:

"Physics teaches us that for every
action, there is an equal and opposite
reaction: a natural balance of energy
that sustains the equilibrium of life.
In modern angling, these forces are
skewed so far in favour of technology
that the balance between science
and art has been lost. But there is
a movement, an undercurrent that
defies the flow of progress. There
are those who choose not to follow
the crowd. They seek not to fish in a
predictable, scientific manner. They
yearn for the opposite, to buck the
trend, *to be different*. They are the
Traditional Anglers."

TRADITIONAL ANGLING

Traditional Angling celebrates the Waltonian values of angling: about fishing in a seasonal and uncompetitive way for the pure pleasure of being beside water. It wears its heart on its sleeve and a wildflower in its lapel. It's passionate, provocative and eccentric, written for those who appreciate the aesthetics of angling and uphold its sporting traditions. So, with great enthusiasm, raise your bamboo rod aloft for an adventure that proves there's more to fishing than catching fish.

READER TESTIMONIALS

"A beautifully written, very engaging and hugely enjoyable read. In fact, it's the best thing on fishing I've read in a long time."

"What a Journal! Fennel is clearly the spiritual successor to his mentor – the great Bernard Venables. There's so much wisdom and craftsmanship in his writing. Bernard clearly taught him very well."

From The Quiet Fields:

"The countryside, with its vast
horizons, fresh air and ever-changing
seasons is, by its very nature, more
life-giving and adventurous than any
amount of modern indoor living.
It inspires a love of natural history –
everything from the birds that sing in
the trees to the quality and richness
of the soil beneath our feet. Most
of all, it creates the desire to exist
more naturally. And in doing so, we
appreciate the balance of life."

NO. 7

THE QUIET FIELDS

The Quiet Fields is rooted in the humus-rich soil of the countryside. It's about remote rural places where Nature exists undisturbed, where we may sit and ponder 'The Wonder of the World'. The Journal tips its hat to these places, and to the nature writing of BB, revealing the 'Lost England' that still exists if you know where and how to look. It is the most sentimental and astutely observed Journal to date, discussing the 'true beauty' of Nature. If you've ever yearned to hear birdsong during a busy day, then this is the book for you.

READER TESTIMONIALS

"Fennel's writing reminds me of the works of Roger Deakin. It inspires me with faith in the quiet life and that although I may be isolated, I am certainly not alone."

"Fennel has captured the essence of the countryside — that is, its almost human character. So brilliantly has he compared and contrasted it with the nature of we humans. It's not so much a 'balanced study', more a 'study of the balance' between Nature and Man."

From Fine Things:

"It seems that, depending upon which side of the thesaurus-writer's gaze we sit, one's uniqueness as a person can be deemed to be either eccentric or distinctive. Both, in my opinion, are good...As we get older, and experience more things, those of us with strength of character and a sense of purpose will grow stronger and fight harder; those who lack identity and direction might end up sitting in a corner somewhere, blindly taking all the knocks that life throws at them. What does this teach us? That character and purpose are directly linked to confidence and conviction. What links them? Courage – to be oneself, no matter what others might say."

NO. 8

FINE THINGS

Fine Things celebrates the special and sentimental items and activities that convey our personality. The writing is fast-paced, quirky and humorous, reflecting the author's enthusiasm and eccentric view of the world. But be warned: if you look inside Fennel's mind, you might see a hula-hooping hamster named Gerald, shaking his maracas, loudly banging a bongo, and getting him into all sorts of trouble. So strap yourself in. This book picks up pace and takes some unexpected turns. From the deeply personal to the outright eccentric, it's for those who seek to be different.

READER TESTIMONIALS

"A very fine thing, indeed. Fennel's best and funniest book to date. He is the only author who can make me laugh out loud and cry in the same sentence. I was constantly in tears, for all the right reasons."

"Deep in places, outright bonkers in others. A demonstration of the fine line between genius and madness."

From A Gardener's Year:

"Roll up your sleeves and imagine
your vision of paradise. This, in
whatever form it takes, is your garden.
Keep hold of the image; know it's
every detail and piece together
the elements that need creating or
nurturing, so that when you get the
chance, you can prepare the ground,
sow the seeds, and make it real.
Ours is a gardener's life, whether we
realise it or not."

NO. 9

A GARDENER'S YEAR

A Gardener's Year celebrates the joy of growing things and reflects upon a life working with plants. But it's not a record of horticultural activities through the seasons. It's a metaphor for having a dream and making it come true. For Fennel, who has spent half his life working in gardens, it's about cultivating a cottage garden where he can aspire to a self-sufficient lifestyle. The Journal sees him sow the seeds of this future reality.

READER TESTIMONIALS

"Fennel's writing is uniquely funny. I mean, who else can name a chapter 'Chicken Poo'? His sense of humour, balanced with some deep yet subtle messages, had me in tears. From his 'escape' to a public toilet, to what not to say to a celebrity, this is a Journal to entertain all readers."

"When I started reading this Journal I had a garden with a lawn and a patio. Now I have a vegetable patch, blisters, an aching back, and the biggest smile of my life. Thank you Fennel!"

From The Lighter Side:

"If self-actualisation is the pinnacle of one's development, then it can't be achieved if your mountain has two peaks...Being the 'best version' of yourself implies that you have other versions kept locked in a closet. Don't have any 'versions'. Just have one true, beautiful and pure form of you.
So climb your mountain, open your arms to the Creator who greets you there, and sing loudly to the world that stretches out beneath you.
Write your name permanently on the landscape of your mind.
Remember: you are a child of Nature. And you are free."

THE LIGHTER SIDE

There's a delicate balance between something meaning a great deal and that same thing becoming so serious that it's ludicrous. (Ever got stressed about what clothes to wear for an interview?) That's why *The Lighter Side* provides the encouragement, humour, anecdotes, reflections and honesty that are essential to Fennel's message of 'Stop – Unplug – Escape – Enjoy'. After all, we can only 'Enjoy' if we know how to smile when we get there.

READER TESTIMONIALS

"The Lighter Side was more than I expected. The deeper meaning within it – and the devastating honesty it conveys – made me question exactly where I am in my own life and what I can do to improve it for my family and me in the time that remains. Thank you Fennel for opening my eyes and adjusting my course."

"The opening chapter is the most startling, erudite, compassionate and open piece of writing I have ever read…thank you Fennel for sharing so much. It did and does mean a great deal."

From Friendship:

"What I'm talking about is proper friendship. The sort that is authentic, genuine and real. Where we can look into the eyes of another person and know what they're thinking. ...Because, as friends, we remember 'why' as much as 'when' or 'what'. Through good times and bad, we were there. Together. That's the bond, the unquestionable obligation that's freely given. It's the tightest hug, the biggest kiss, the tearful hello and the widest smile. If that's what it means to be a friend, or an extrovert, or just someone who cares for others then that's me to the last beat of my heart."

NO. 11

FRIENDSHIP

Written by the Friends of the Priory, with bonus chapters from Fennel, *Friendship* provides insights into what it means to be friends, how shared interests and beliefs support collective purpose, and how, when we're together, we can achieve more, appreciate more, and have more fun. It's about the broader world of Fennel's Priory and how it exists in others. It's a book that's 'for us by us', with friendship as the overall theme.

READER TESTIMONIALS

"Possibly the greatest gift that this Journal bestows is to let us know that we are not alone."

"Like friendship itself, this Journal brings together people and meaning. It reminds us that 'together we are strong'. Thank you Fennel for leading our charge."

"The message (and evolution) of Fennel's Journal is most evident in this Friendship edition. With such obvious themes as identity and legacy, it's clear that what Fennel has shared over the years is a route-map to freedom and a stronger sense of self."

From Nature Escape:

"I am once again seeking an escape,
to where I hope to find freedom and
connect with the young man who
handed me his trust ten years ago.
This will be a faithful interpretation
of the Priory, and a fitting way to
mark ten years of writing.
As I said at the end of last year's
Journal, 'One's journey through life
is not linear; it's circular.'
So let's go back to the beginning,
and rediscover the quiet world."

NO. 12

NATURE ESCAPE

Nature Escape provides the most detailed account of a day that follows the motto of 'Stop – Unplug – Escape – Enjoy'. In it Fennel returns to the woodland of his youth to study its wildlife and savour its peacefulness.

Written in real-time, with twenty-four chapters that each represent an hour, the Journal is an account of how time spent outdoors in wild places enables us to observe the nature that's around us *and* within us.

READER TESTIMONIALS

"Fennel's Journal has always provided us with an escape, but now we know where the escape can lead. As promised, it leads to enjoyment – and very enjoyable it is too!"

"24 hours alone in a wood, with only 'the wild' for company? With Fennel as our guide, there's no such thing as 'alone'; only the warmth of knowing that quiet times are the fine times."

"By studying the nature within us and around us, Fennel demonstrates how to be 'at one' with nature."

From Book of Secrets:

"There's a greater man than me
who can sum up our journey, a
mountaineer who in 1865 first
climbed the Matterhorn. Edward
Whymper, over to you: 'There have
been joys too great to be described
in words, and there have been griefs
upon which I have not dared to dwell,
and with these in mind I say, climb if
you will, but remember that courage
and strength are naught without
prudence, and that a momentary
negligence may destroy the happiness
of a lifetime. Do nothing in haste,
look well to each step, and from
the beginning think what may
be the end.'"

NO. 13

BOOK OF SECRETS

Book of Secrets links all editions of Fennel's Journal together. With 14 Journals in the series, and 14 core chapters in this book, it's the 'one book to bind them all' with each chapter providing the continuity story from one Journal to the next.

Containing Fennel's previously private writing, it provides deep insight into the Fennel's Journal story. If you've ever wondered why each Journal is themed the way it is, or tried to find the metaphor in each edition, then *Book of Secrets* is for you.

READER TESTIMONIALS

"What a privilege: being able to read the private writing of my favourite author. Book of Secrets is a treat."

"Such honesty and wit. Fennel puts into words what I have only ever thought, or dare not say."

"Fennel's Journal really is a series – it's meant to be read as a whole. And now we have the key to unlock it."

From The Pursuit of Life:

"We can hide, or we can strive – for a life of our making. With endless possibilities and opportunities to reach for our dreams, we owe it to ourselves to dream big and keep going, irrespective of what we might encounter. Sadly, the thing that most limits our success is not others, but ourselves. How strongly we believe, how confidently we act, how fiercely we react, how passionately we want, and how life-affirmingly compelled we are to grow and blossom; that's how we keep going, no matter what, to be the person we want to be, living the life we deserve, in dreams that are real."

NO. 14

THE PURSUIT OF LIFE

The Pursuit of Life concludes the Fennel's Journal story. It's a reflective tome that provides Fennel's commentary on the journey and a 'behind the scenes' view of the challenges and rewards of a life rebuilt on one's terms.

It's an account of how the series came to be and how it evolved, and includes much of Fennel's private writing, several of the original handwritten drafts, correspondence between The Friends, and encouragement for those on similar paths. Ultimately it shows how the Fennel's Journal series can be used as a route map to a more fulfilling life.

READER TESTIMONIALS

"A life retold, for our benefit. Fennel is to be congratulated for everything he's achieved – on paper and in life."

"It's his life in the books, but it could so very easily be ours. Fennel has a way of seeing truth in the severe and the sublime, and bringing it home."

"Can this really be the end? When dreams are real, we never wake from them. More books Fennel, please!"

Lightning Source UK Ltd.
Milton Keynes UK
UKHW040941080219
336898UK00001B/172/P

9 781909 947238